Praise for *If But My Gaze Could Heal*

"Colin Greer is in conversation with some of the greats and he is holding his own."—**Dr. Cornel West**, professor, philosopher, author, activist

"When Wallace Stevens proclaimed, 'In poetry, you must love the words, the ideas and the images and rhythms with all your capacity to love anything at all,' he could have been describing Colin Greer's astonishing collection *If But My Gaze Could Heal*. In poem after poem, Greer gob smacks us with an imagination in overdrive that leaves us reeling with characters, philosophies, perspectives, and metaphors that dance dervishly across lines that won't stand still. Yet, he occasionally gives us a breather to ponder aphoristic wisdom like 'I've read grace fills empty spaces./So there's hope even if stars burn out,' and it 'Takes time to look, to see, to turn up the heat.' This rich and intriguing collection requires taking time, time to gaze with the poet as 'The Earth quakes/Ready to take one for the team/If we can learn/to listen.' A hallmark of Greer's art, this book ignites the heat of surprise, awe, and, if we listen closely enough, the grace in empty spaces."—**Carolyn Martin, Ph.D.**, Poet and Poetry Editor of *Kosmos Quarterly: Journal for Global Transformation*

"There is a longing in this poet-activist, who sees more than we can bear, but mirth and joy are part of the seeing and it draws us there."—**Matt Weiner**, Associate Dean, Office of Religious Life at Princeton University

"Being the body and voice for 'Treaty Between Self and Earth' poems was without a doubt one of the deepest and most exciting challenges of my acting career. My soul was touched by every single word, giving me the opportunity to make an even deeper connection with the piece and give layers and colors to the character. Such strong and delicate matter, translated in the most beautiful and poetic way possible is a true gift for me as an actor and I'll be forever grateful for the opportunity to experience and embody something so incredibly special."—**Alice Reis**, actor, singer, dancer

"Gripping, suspenseful and funny in a way that few poets are—Greer has managed to create something quite rare and extraordinary: a page turner. His writing about politics reminds one of what is important in everyday life, and his writing about everyday life could motivate you to enter politics. His poetry is almost deceptively easy to read. The author has a rhythm and ease that invites us to sit down, as if for a casual conversation with a friend—only to then find yourself enjoying a deeper discourse on the meatiest and toughest subjects in American public life—power, class, race, politics. And just when we get comfortable talking, he moves us to stand up and act."—**Svante Myrick**, Executive Director of People For the American Way

"I love this collection of poems—it is a book I will keep by my side always. When I read Colin Greer's poetry, I hear music. And then I close my eyes and see images, vivid images, that linger and dance above consciousness. I travel from the future to the ancient past with astonishing stops along the way that dare me to open my eyes to think about the world in ways I never thought possible."—**N. Scott Johnson**, architect, artist, musician, composer

"Reading Colin's poetry is much like standing in between two mirrors in an attic: I face the multitudes of humanity—from beauty to brutality—in a mise an abyme of ghost stories. This particular collection gifts us a sliver of hope for breaking the curse. A sobering, hands-in-the-dirt kind of hope - the only kind I trust these days. Nothing left to think about, they tell me, time to dive in."—**Esther Meroño Baro,** community organizer and multimedia artist

"These evocative poems examine the human condition in all of its wonder and all of its failings. At turns erudite and terrestrial, Greer's voice implores the reader to look closer, to draw connections, to fly from branch to branch, and we do."—**Emma Straub,** author of *This Time Tomorrow*

IF BUT
MY GAZE
COULD HEAL

Poetry by
Colin Greer

LANTERN PUBLISHING & MEDIA | WOODSTOCK & BROOKLYN, NY

2022
PO Box 1350
Woodstock, NY 12498
www.lanternpm.org

Cover design by Rebecca Moore
Copyediting by Pauline Lafosse

Printed in the United States of America

Library of Congress Cataloging-in-Publication Data

Names: Greer, Colin, author.
Title: If but my gaze could heal : a book of poems / Colin Greer.
Description: Woodstock, NY : Lantern Publishing & Media, 2022.
Identifiers: LCCN 2022007840 (print) | LCCN 2022007841 (ebook) |
    ISBN 9781590566688 (hardcover) | ISBN 9781590566695 (ebook)
Subjects: LCGFT: Poetry.
Classification: LCC PS3607.R46986 I4 2022 (print) | LCC PS3607.
    R46986 (ebook) | DDC 811/.6—dc23/eng/20220321
LC record available at https://lccn.loc.gov/2022007840
LC ebook record available at https://lccn.loc.gov/2022007841

All with thanks and admiration for Simone Weil for her belief and witness that a loving and just gaze can relieve suffering.

CONTENTS

Dedication xiii
Acknowledgments xv
Foreword: Rev Billy Talen xvii

BOOK I: WITH OR WITHOUT WHICH 1
With or Without Which 2
War 4
Resistance 5
Peasant Work 7
Fascism 8
Darlings 9
He Walks His Dog 10
Elementary Teaching 11
Question Emoji 13
In the Know 14
A New-Fashioned Walk 15
In the Stars 17
Bewilderment 18
Candle Rituals 20
My Mind in a Stew 21
Burning Bush 22
If But My Gaze Could Heal 23

BOOK II: MISCHIEF AND MELANCHOLY 25
Love Sonnet 26
They Write 27
Plato 29
On the Street 31

Forecast 32

Angola 1 of 3 34

Confession Found on a Seat 36

Truth 37

Thoughts and Ideas 38

Creation 39

Radio Daze 40

When the Earth Turned Round 42

Revolution and Art 44

Swinging Ideas 45

Mischief and Melancholy 46

Ridiculous Man 47

W.E.B. 48

One Giant Leap 49

Doubt Can be a Problem 50

Flying Paper 51

Souls in the Lower Circles 52

BOOK III: STICK OUT YOUR TONGUE 53

Goons with Guns 54

There are no Tanks 56

7/14/20 57

Some Things Have Changed (After Brecht) 58

Stick Out Your Tongue 60

Think/Imagine 61

Simone Weil Wrote 64

Roots 65

Humanity on Trial 66

Unless and Until 68

Big Bang/Big Question 70

Country Club Bigots 71

Playtime 72

Kept In 73

Common Good 74

Protest Neat a Catskill Cemetery 75

Tyranny Redux   76
Walking Backwards   77
Addicted   78

BOOK IV: PHEW!   79
Phew!   80
Poem for Another Day   81
Mystery of Love   83
Stranger with a Familiar Face   84
Lord Nelson   85
Shape of the World   86
Hoody   87
So Long a Border   88
Macadam   89
Elements of Striving   90
Keeping Warm   92
Schism   93
Taking Off   94
Balance   95
What is a Good Story   96
East/West   98
Yellow Livered   99
Three Fifths   101
Hand to Mouth   107
Sophia   108
Survivors   112
Turning Point   117
Looking for our Equal   118
The Body Politic   119
Hope   120
The Reproduction of Shame   121
Sound and Light Frequencies   122
Carcass   124
Same Old Same Old   125
Bun and Burger   126

Imagine You are Coached by an Angel   127
All is Well   129
Natural Allies   135

BOOK V:
    WHAT IS HIDDEN AND HIDDEN FROM   137
Convention   138
The Hitch   140
The Way We R   142
What is Hidden and Hidden From   144
There Will be a Time When   146
Relatively Speaking   149
Why Children's Authors Anthropomorphize
    Animals and Flowers   151
I Came Upon   153
When I Courted Atheism in Eden   155
Flat Earth   157
Articles I II and III of Treaty Between Earth and Self
    (With Preambles)   158
Mapping   161
Epiphany   163
Lateral Formations   167
Oskar Morgenstern Vs Bowling Alone   170
Sigmund to Albert   171
I Twinkling   172
Beauty/Truth Truth/Beauty   173
The Stickiness of Fly Paper   176
When Earth Quakes   185
No Bounds   187
Sun in a Twist   188

About the Author
About the Publisher

DEDICATION

To the healers.

I have been healed in my life by the people I've been blessed to know. We have shared work, making the workplace joyful, and we have been helpmates along the way, making life rich in empathy and laughter.

These healers all resisted self-importance while working to reverse conditions that bring people down into the quagmire of indignity and coercion. Yet without demeaning those who demean others because, as I have learned from them, there is no wellbeing in denigration of persons.

From them I have learned to take energy from anger, and compassion from humiliation. They each have known the deepest parts of themselves and recognize that there is only so much they can actually know of others. They were each ennobled in their recognition of the tightrope we walk just getting dressed each morning one foot at a time.

I list the names of these wonderful people, because all too often quiet tenderness and faithfulness go unrecognized: Barry Sherman, Gerry Epstein, Sabe Basescu, Martin Kassan, Sophia Bracy-Harris, Peggy Saika, Patricia Wilson, Hubert and Jane Sapp, Karen Bass, Madeline Adamson, Bena Kallick, Frank Reissman, Ross Evans, Hayward Burns, Charles Hey-Maestre, Linda Colon.

ACKNOWLEDGEMENTS

Thanks to Brian Normoyle who made the possibility of this book real and helped it develop, Rebecca Erwin has edited as well as typed, she has checked punctuation and been an ever-alert reader, and Esther Meroño Baro who has made many of these poems available on my blog and enhanced them with beautifully evocative photographs.

Thanks to Alnoor Ladha who read my work and brought it to the attention of Carolyn Martin at Kosmos Journal, and to Rev Billy Talen at the Church of Stop Shopping. Two relationships that have become important to me and keep evolving.

Scott Johnson who heard music in four poems (Mapping, Epiphany, In the Know, and Treaty Between Self and Earth), and brought put his cello to work, creating beautiful music and leading to an ensemble of artists (Danilo Gambini, Jody Sperling, Alice Reys, Victor Caccese) to create dance, voice, and percussion, for a stage performance launched at the Rattlestick Playwrights Theater in New York City.

Thanks to my family, kids, and grandkids who inspire me; their voices and embraces are another kind of poetry. My wife Franny is always my first reader, and her input always opens up expansive possibilities.

FOREWORD

REV BILLY TALEN

In the apocalyptic explosion of this present moment, how does an artist hold a steady gaze? How do you get a good long look at the landscape around you, when the fire and flood rage, when the big institutions withdraw from everyday life of people, and the ultimate shadow of extinction touches all of life?

The answer, in theory, would be that to make a comment on life you would have to be in motion yourself, such that the blurring debris flying by is suddenly standing still and clear because you yourself are moving with the explosion. Colin Greer attempts to create such a dance, with lines and stanzas that whizz by and create a stillness. In fact, I've never read poems that leave my head in such motion, as in the act of a double-take. What happened? But then the momentary "what?" makes the second look more deeply vivid.

He will cruise along and then abruptly leap, then turn around and address us point blank with unpressured conversation. And then, after that, there might be vivid lines of poetry that give off a metallic blue color to hypnotic effect, and wham, he nails us with an epigram you could carve in marble.

The Jackson Pollock crossed with fizzy bubble tea that Colin Greer creates leaves us with an intimate knowledge of chaos. We trust him at the same time that we want to catch him. He races, weaves, skates, and escapes. He is confident in his flights, and never seems to let us conclude that he is lost or overwhelmed by the mysterious, just clever.

His gambit is that he will teach a form that we must learn on the spot, with dance-steps that sometimes feel impossible. His language spirals, stops, looks at you, then gallops away and dares you to stay safe in the meaning of the phrase you thought you understood. Maybe it's easier to understand a difficult truth, like the violent fracture of the human project, when the writer has induced in us a state of shock.

How do we loaf and invite our soul in 2022? Greer can wear the human race lightly, but he'll fly into the darkness soon enough. He doesn't loaf, and he doesn't suffer the predictable gladly. Let me offer the first three and last three lines of a poem near the end of the book called "Mapping." It's the aesthete suddenly caught in the weeds and monsters of racism.

I like what is called mapping
Drawing routes, light years, roads
Not yet travelled, the micro future

———————

And oh...
I map the tremblings of monsters
Who run their mouths on emptiness
In hope some terrifying Other might make them human

Greer seems to be carrying a weightless page of wisdom from somewhere in the old I-Thou and applying it to all of us, to our public space. Or you might say "public page." There is a constant gravity in his poems to find a place to speak, while the destroyed commons is actually hunting him down, to silence his singing thoughts.

I'm defining the speaker's corner as the bullhorn we can no longer pick up. But that place for the voice could be the Principia Mathematica or The Clash but it was the place where speech and was introduced, and is largely banned now—or, in the US, mocked by products. The commons competes with Consumerism and Militarism, strong institutions or sometimes strong men, and always a Shopper's Channel added through society-wide brain surgery.

Here in New York the concentration of armed police in public space is constantly self-valorizing. Greer is making the new public space in the air, outmaneuvering the fake electronic commons, the altar calls, the security zones. I mention the altar because, one way of looking at this poet's honest address of conditions is that he is fighting religious fundamentalism. While the modern economy pretends it has replaced the God's Law of the colonial times, actually the upgrade is mostly style shifting. The big difference is that the religio-economy of today has banned its Book of Revelations because extinction is actual and unmonetized.

Indeed, how do you loaf and invite your poem in the vertigo of the Sixth Great Extinction? You find that seam in public space and cultivate your love and tenderness there like you've found your garden. Either that or you stun yourself with pixels, billboards the size of tsunamis, fungible art converted to unknown currencies, solar-powered marital devices, pesticides that manager your biome.... Greer is taking on that landscape of fatal trash coming to life.

He's opening up new public space by adroitly treating the in-betweenness, cultivating what was passed over, the deep-mapper.

Greer makes the unusual choice to bypass professionalized perspective. He's like an ordinary person with a fast brain; eyes open with a big heart. So he trusts the inventions of our community of author and reader.

It's in the ordinary, trusting friend in a neighborhood shared with the reader that he assumes permission to yank us around, drop us and fly us over, stop us in mid-sentence and let the abyss look up at the mountain. There's pleasure in how scary this writing is, because it's not based on fear, or technique. In this time of extinction, it's a gift to share that scared world we actually live in. Have the adventure of this book!

I'll end this foreword with the first lines of a poem midway in the book, another homage of sorts to Simone Weil.

Simone Weil: so long as we are in struggle
Against evil, each bit of evil we destroy grows up
Again as before.

Ouch!
Splat!

Can one, a person I mean, be a saint
And live past 33?
Can a person live to thirty-five
Without an ego?

Can a person check ego at the bar
And survive a gunfight?

Boom!
Bam!

Rev Billy Talen
The Church of Stop Shopping
New York

BOOK I:

WITH OR WITHOUT WHICH

"How one would love to be able to leave one's soul in the little box where one places one's clocking ticket, and take it up again upon leaving!"

(Simone Weil)

With or Without Which

With regard to things seen
Proportion enables the soul
        to grasp
All at once
A multiplicity of points of view
        without which
It would lose itself
Exiled in time and space.

All the methods of proportion
Are simple techniques for freeing the soul
From the effects of time
        so that
It may come to feel
        almost at home
In its place of exile,
        happy
In the situation of one little human body
In the world
Where the lines in the sand are cracked
Due to the tide
        with which
Neptune rusts canon.

A lone dog wails   eagles circle
Winds blow gravel into roiling
                    wicked shrugs
Of history's   complex variety
Uncontrolled   unlimited.

It is a natal necessity to find
Regularity in diversity
                    to locate proportion.
Then little human bodies in the world
Waiting for god
                    can sun.
Without which
                    the soul is divided
By thought,
Like a lone dog wailing.

War

Soldiers weary back
with fractured fontanelles
open to the urge to wave   old
bloody blame again....
The knot that binds,
and the not that can release love
from terror, grace from truth.

Resistance

Deer in the headlights: Done.
Lungs burst into lobes not known yet,
Stomach lining blows out like dust in a whirlwind.
The production line holds, rounded
By electrified wire.

Inside jobs offer multiplier effects.
War meanders in traffic of despair
And the maples have already turned red.

Kick up your heels, call gravity a liar,
Trust is the silent syllable.
In kindness,
Doubt hovers like pinwheels in a light wind.

Thirst and hunger will be sated
Frozen pipes and empty bread bins
Make shadows of us all.

Dark mornings and black evenings
Sandwich the days without windows.
The only natural reflex is repetitive motion
And dehydration.

Keel over in a make-do kitchen
Your dizzying fear is ravenous:
Who is to cup your head
        and stroke your hair?

Look around   crawl to the exit
If no one sees   no one   is there
If no one is there how can you be free?

Surely what you long for has a face,
Cantabile in the blood is scrambled
As if a giant juicer squeezed out the flavor.

Only groaning in Handel's chorus
Phlegm at vespers

Resistance is how we know about the world.

Peasant Work

Coffee aroma should not smell like a funeral pyre.
It does when involuntary memory sips into mind.

Waking up is not a simple equation, no simple interest
Loitering in the poker deck.

Likewise cotton balls and cereal corn cornered
By bamboo imports and redolent redwoods.
The cumulae of a quick puff on a cigarette or two.

Fascism

A yearning
gone wrong.
    yearning
filled with flattery

high regard for
supreme leaders,
faces on flags
worship wins

dissidents were once nailed
    by their tongues
in neighbors' doors. Later
one hand one foot is nailed
on a cross
    to cajole
with no prospect of redemption.

Darlings

(How Simone addressed her parents)

My father told me never to tell a woman
"I love you." I never heard him or my mother say it.

They stood for hours, packed boxes,
Carried and delivered them. They grew bent
Like a heron's neck folded in a hungry whirl.

Love spoken might compel comparisons
With yesterday or some other time.

Better quotidian silence, coded sign language
For yeomen affection. Unspoken
Might be a prompt to dream
Or incur yet more nightmare lacerations.

Smoky clouds rolling in like family saying
What kind of day this was, what's next.
Until you have to laugh as in all lucky families.

Question is, can grace catch up with desire
On the run around the Grecian urn?

He Walks his Dog

He walks his dog as the sun clocks out.
He told me he spends each day waiting to live.
Twilight is his most beautiful time: a fragment of the truth.

His dog barks once, a soft endorsement.
Nothing to prove, she shakes her head
To lead him to the dock.

Elementary Teaching

A kayak on its side
(still calls itself canoe at times)
Is bleeding invisible ink
Praying for the sun to make blood visible
Without any interest in tanning.
Inside, detritus floating in stagnant water
Moccasins, sandals, sneakers
Diverse DNA decomposing.

Kindergarten lesson: decomposition means
Return to earth.

What might we compose instead?

500 year old trees lose branches
Without malice.
A child's comfort blanket tears in play
Without regret.
Unattributed ideas that spark new thought
Generate rustler claims.
A child walking at 5 months, talking at 3 years
Is credit or a blow to parents.

This is what September looks like
Sun sets earlier than last week
Elections are 60 days away

Some birds are out ahead to scout
New beaches, squawking like flaps
On a box decomposing in morning mist.

What might we compose instead?

Fire will extinguish itself by late fall
Most children will walk and talk soon enough
Ideas like water in pipes will run into watershed
And slag.   Some futures can be seen.

Kindergarten lesson: prediction means
Guessing what the future looks like.

Fleas still carry bubonic plague
Drivers swerve around roadkill
Without stopping. Jews look for safety
In prayer shawl pajamas. Never again
Is rife in all ears. Control is never ceded
To victims.

Kindergarten lesson: a victim is evidence
That somebody has won.

What might we compose instead?

Question Emoji

The heron is an animated question mark:
Why who what when,
You mean now?

Stretching its head the heron answers
Its own question:
Of course now.

When I look up from taking the note
The sentence is concluded, period:
The heron has flown.

In the Know

You know how a baby propels arms
Toward heaven, aiming to stand, but not yet.
You know how the heron propels her wings
To the stars into flight, but not for long.
You know how rabbits scamper about
Like fluff off a dandelion, stop to play statue,
Then chase their tails.

These are known knowns
      and you are in the know.

You know barn raising is what neighbors do.
Like refusing to let the planet burn or drown.
You know to calm a woman's grief,
Put her tears in your hanky, replace her torn leather
Soles and her boy's frayed nylon knickers.
You can haul the two-by-fours, hammer the nails,
Sweat in just the way the good lord intended.
That's what neighbors do.
You know what they say about walking on by
Closing yourself in. If you haven't heard
They say it's the beginning of sin. You must know
About barn raising, it's what neighbors do.

These are known knowns
      and you are in the know.

A New-Fashioned Walk

A poem and a song took a walk
To agree
      on 1 or 2
      challenges
To the cannon's roar.

The poem parsed philosophy
With a gentle shrug between words.
The song evoked fortune cookies
      in f
      sharp

And donut went contrapuntal
      dis
      harmony
Until a serpent hanging from an apple tree

Offered fruit
      as they
      do.
The poem said I've been here before
The song found it a bit of a bore.
The serpent offered the song
      a 2nd
      look

The poem considered:
    1 bad
    apple.

Then surprise, the song bit off
    the serpent's
    head.
The poem kneeled in deep respect
    an eternal
    bow.

In the Stars

For a flotsam Jew assault continues to happen.
No one experience of it more true than another.
For jetsam Blacks, the pain continues to happen.
In light years there's the story of the pain.

Believing it will stop continues to happen too.
In the flame of a star on   its brightest nights
Repair may already exist. Short of that
You might as well be a squirrel.

See it dodging around political placards
In an early snow to avoid traffic. Just remember
Where the nuts are buried. Like thoughts
They are objects primed to meet other objects.

According to some brain scientists unfamiliar
With astrology, translation, or hermeneutics.
Re-read, re-write, kick open the gate,
Hobble through.
The soap box is slippery, but never mind.

I've read grace fills empty spaces.
So there's hope even if stars burn out.

Bewilderment

To cleave to a comfort object
Is the heaven of childhood:
Affection and control.

The doll or blanket almost as verifiably alive
As the child's lucky embrace of abundance.
Her mind as swinging as a mobile

She is centered on herself:
Might a wink move an object?
Can a hand without a name
Reach the thing yet without a name?

Meanwhile...
There is walking
Teething.
The sun in her hands.
Skin peeling in the corner of her thumb
At the cuticle.

Hands making and spending,
The trick that turns fingers into people
Gathered in a church.

In the light of the stained glass
There is grandeur in a crowd
Bathed in the bewilderment

Of mobile stigmata.
You can sniff the punchline coming.

The sun in her hands.
Skin peeling in the corner of her thumb
At the cuticle.

My dictionary has ripped its pages!
scrambled all its words,
like a father teaching a child to skip stones
as the sun comes up

I watch the sun go down
and Om.
While I Om the impatient sun
leaves.

In the radiating glow I see deer
loping in the water, dolphins chasing
in the car park, angels nursing babies
without regard to species.

Candle Rituals

Can we be enchanted enough to survive?

Are we waiting for the candle to blow out?
Are our fingers shaking, shot through with a universal
Gehrig's disease?

As one by one people return to earth
Is overpopulation going to kick up too much dust
At the back end? Can the drip drip of wax,
The sensation of blood lapping on life, evolve us?
Can we live better together?

No!
We've been lighting candles for thousands of years,
What are we waiting for?

Yes!
That's right.
We are waiting for ourselves.

My Mind In A Stew

When I remember milk teeth...

Yes, ownership was with the breeders by law.
International treaties made it so everywhere
In fields and factories pretty faces were worn out petals
before very long.

Rickets, iron filings in mothers' milk,
Her food for a month no more than an appetizer
at Nice Matin.

Tip and tail green beans
In the big house kitchen,
I'm trying to see more clearly.
There is a smell in my eyelids
from the grass at the shore after the tide,
like Spinoza choking on glass particles.

Burning Bush

I see an angry cat high in the bush
Beating against my window. Or is it a fox?

I walked behind a man on crutches, stood by him
At the curb. He turned, no sir not crutches
These are wings with which I beat the air.

Another man chewing on his thoughts.
Follows my gaze up to stare
At the man in the moon who seems to have dropped
     a rung or two.

I am here because the beating stopped.
I am here because the cat was soothed.
I am here because a bush caught fire,
Under the colors and sounds of vanity.

If But My Gaze Could Heal

I am not a doctor nor a cab driver
Who delivers babies insisting
On being born now.

I am not a detective nor EMS
Who follow the smoke
To rescue suicides.

I have no perp I "like"
No kiss of life expertise
I am the suicide I am the baby.

Neurologist tells me to touch my nose
Right hand forefinger then left
My nose points its own way to you.

Perception reflex good on all counts
Despite the heavy rain
I notice primroses on the bank

Duck into shade
To flower again
Aching to be born.

If but my gaze could heal
I'd do this all day.

        not so odd for a man

To put on red shoes
And long for Kansas.

BOOK II:
MISCHIEF AND MELANCHOLY

*"Translating means serving two masters. It follows
that no one can do it."*

(Hans-Georg Gadamer)

Love Sonnet,

Soil and soul share roots
Except when soil means spoil.

Old seat of learning
Now roof tiles flap like lids
In a wc.

Applicants who could love
Were admitted here.
They scored high on a love test.
No one could ever claim high performance
After graduating, love takes no credit.

Finally Subaru hired graduates
For TV ads and "have a nice day" jingles.

The college closed years back
Unexpectedly some would say.
But they would be wrong.

They Write

They write that the   world will get better
Or worse.
And how,
Against whom,
With whose effort.
They write about the need for small,
The need for large,
For global,
For local,
For rural,
With some shopping close by,
Some walkways,
Some cities,
No cities,
No elevators,
Better elevators.
Old woods,
Better woods.
They write no more gas,
More wind,
More broadband,
More work,
And less work.

They write about the newest meaning,
Of fingers walking, the old meaning rotting.
What won't rot, you live with.
They write to recommend:
Point like a baby,
Exercise your fingers,
Don't crack your knuckles.

Plato

Soaz is an uncertain friend
Good days and bad.
Like war, migraines are always coming
Warning signs easily missed.
When go-to-bed, sleep it off,
Might have helped,
> the head blows up
> on the sidewalk.

> Kiricki!
> Kiricki!

The cock crows insurrection
And reform/nation
Crown over clavier
Gospel loses
Tell Mephistopheles the NBA is canceled
Fausted
The blindfold can come off.

> Kiricki!
> Kiricki!

There is a gun in a cherry wood drawer
Wrapped in a linen handkerchief.
Comfort for the pistol's endless pain,
Masquerading as a short answer
To long long questions.

                                        Kiricki!
                                        Kiricki!

Persons can shelter in an anagram
Like words do: words in words,
Bodies in bodies.

Plato returned to class for an oral interview:
"Shadow, sir?"
"Caves will do that. As sapiens climbs
 Shadows lie in wait."
"Ideal, sir?"
"Sapiens failing is sapiens unhidden,
 The sapiens-ness of sapiens" he said
 Letting himself out.

Scarlet ribbon falls to the ground
Writhing as it takes the shape of wind
Like an elephant stropping on empty.
The flaw in the rug is us who walk on it.

On The Street

On the street: oxygen!
Give me oxygen!

Phlogiston is a killer theory
For cold air.

Running in my brain
    again and again.
Why can't we get along?
    so long   so long
Plus ça change, it's Treyvon
All over again.
Crosses with roses
Crosses with rotting souls
Of carpenters who've never slept in a barn,
Birthed by mothers who hum like queen bees
"Honey, you gotta get them else they gonna get us."
And the other mothers bearing white sons
Who'll say "honey, what have I not said?
What must I do to unburden your heart
    into the whirlwind?"
Like a rubber band unscrewing frozen jars.

Forecast

Cold 20-30 degrees
    rain showers
mixed periodically with wet snow.

Thought: the rain will be damp too.
Then there's Bach conducting my wipers.

No cell service, no street lights,
    a certain immunity.
Radio news: new scope reveals 3 billion new galaxies.
Thought: three not 2.9 billion, not 3.1.

Traffic ahead, 3 car pileup.
    sledding on wet roads
    estimated 1 hour to clear.
Thought: for some there will be no clear.

Then: Zenzile Makeba pumps Dylan
    through the rattle.
Radio news: Musk says if it takes a coup
    do a coup.

Not immunity, a certain exposure...
Heavy blowing snow now expected,
    near blizzard conditions.
High volume of precipitation, and
    very wet snow
      going to be a big one.

Radio news: UFO study shows aliens
    prefer the cold, cold and dry.
Thought: just yesterday I prayed for rain,
And the kids begged for snow.

Angola 1 of 3

6 x 9 in NYC runs about $1000 per month.
In Louisiana blood boils in 54 feet sq.
The bars are molten
Strains of plastic forks on them
Are orchestrated by who knows who
For a full measure of melancholy.

40 years in one room is a fetid sauna
For immigrant sewers, machine and cottons
On the toilet seat. In Angola state prison
40 years is all the time and no time
After choice retracts like a rubber band
Unscrewing frozen jars.

Reading in a sweatshop is all direction and detail.
In solitary it's about opening old cans,
Maybe the sardines are edible.
Brothers for keepers, stretched cortex
                              and soul food
To Albert. Mr. Woodfax to himself.
Hoarded pics in his cones running   on a spool:
The   Collyer house on 138th Street. He took in
Each room and window, every football field
On 5 floors before the handcuffs.

In Angola he ran reran and reran the pics.
45 years later he sits on a bench
                              in the pocket park
After the house, where stacks of newsprint
Once crowded a few Steinway pianos
                              and a model T.

Confession Found On A Seat

Propelled up and down by anger
Not hunger
My projects all fashioned to rip a new hole
In someone's arse.
Every one of them failed
In flips and flops.
Practice in the game of getting and forgetting,
Piety on the wall with Humpty.
Splat!
Like Adam in the muck of it.
It was all flour and water,
Not oil,
The possibility of baking
Without a recipe.
I wanted to be unleavened,
Without any sacred code.
Unleaven me!

Truth

The Hudson River School is all about light.
Some would say it's all about truth
On a palette finding its home in the eye
Of the painter and in sapiens.

I ask myself if truth is an allergen for some
I tell myself I've seen people react badly
I wonder if I've seen enough to know.
I imagine it varies: the truth and the allergen.

I hear a thunder base claiming truth is truth,
No ship without an anchor
Then it rains. The tears sink in
For all the dead soldiers, the unknown warriors,
The starving children, the battered women,
The policemen with ischemic eruptions
After pulling the trigger impulsively.

Thoughts and Ideas

I planned to leave my thoughts to science
And to give my best ideas to transplant candidates
Waiting on edge for a new perspective.

I've been asked if I think my ideas
Will, like a marrow transplant, bring my blood
Into another's stream of consciousness.

And I wish I knew.
I'll have to give that question
More thought.

Creation

The color on the condo is faded
After just two years, maybe three.
Weather is a tyrannical artist.

Tempera dries quickly.
Painters have to plan in advance,
Maybe using a single color in several scenes.
Only then comes another color.

The creation story so often used
To beg the palette question:
Did god wait long enough? Did god spread evil across
All His explosive endeavors?

Jacob Lawrence got it all right in Toussaint
And the migration series. Chagall on Cathedral windows.

Fear of the police in Harlem, fear of being in a pogrom,
Both lived in the extended civil wars that freed them.
Can any painter
Liberate the Lord?

Radio Daze

He sits at the mic spouting platitudes
In the currency on bliss:
"When you're right, you're right
And right you are to listen to me."

Tautology is an Eden of promise,
East of collapse. The gardener competes
With the rain. His roses snigger and pout
Under glass.

A past with a hint of presence
Lived reality in a fun house
Carnival logic chattering through false teeth
Dehydration chokes air out of his speech.

Not yet the last syllable of recorded time
Still and all, transcordant exchange
Of fleece pillows for rocks and barnacles.
The temptation of temptation:
No less natural than rambling trees is a case of stairs.

Before you bang your head
On the floor, pile up some pillows.
Either way you bounce, padding helps.
Stand on them if you prefer,
Gain height like Everest. Depends only
On what's counted and who counts.
Then again, losing height is an option
Like ice caps melting.

His confidence is on a shilling meter now.
He's not taking calls. He squints at the moon,
It can afford to lose a sliver of its ¾ fullness tonight.
And, he like the sun, must pause
To change direction.

When the Earth Turned Round

The secret life of a polite secret life
Ends if the camera is on when it's not
Supposed to be.

Misstep on a board boozed up
The drunken sop is a public fool
Not so supposed to be.

Secrets lived in public, like frogs torn
Out of tadpoles still *in flagrante*
National geographic body cams full on.

Throw in the towel, but dry it first
Wring it out. Perhaps once cried
Defeat will be defeated, embarrassment satisfied.
The colors will run and it won't matter
Because music travels fast through water,
Even in distress, there can be harmony.

The secret life of unsaintly people
Like trees with loping limbs,
Skin peeling, age showing (am I writing
About trees again?) in public view.
Too lone swimmers might throw towels and clothes
Over a branch in a state park to lay naked
Like Noah, water dripping, water always giving
      information
To the ordinary eye.

All of a flutter in the breeze, ice forms, water about and
    below 32°
Giving the impression of one more year to reach
The saintly span of Jesus, Simone
And the sacred private lives and deaths of unknown
    saints.

When the world was flat
Attempted inattentive sapiens
Could
Just
Fall
Off.
Knowing what one knows
Is
Nothingness, that is
Being
On
Being.
In the ways it is
When the world is round.

Revolution and Art

Milton liked the Thames
Thinking about revolution.
Wordsworth walks around his lake
Revolution at the back of his mind:
> *Divine drama*
> *Nature's numina.*

Thoreau's mind whirled in the woods
(Breakfast came with Mom)
Dreaming of sapiens' freedom
(And breakfast every morning).

Children watch
Without looking
The way Beethoven wrote his concerti
Without hearing.
Rilke shattered sin
Whiplashed evil:
The foundation of art.

Camus trusted art.
Benjamin had faith in it.
Camus on a bike
Benjamin in the Pyrenees
Both fragments
Of two big stones, off Sinai.
They each made a great escape from virtue
That chains the wrists and ankles of multitudes.

Swinging Ideas

Like an acrobat folding and unfolding
Deconstructionists contend with hermeneutists.
Grounded meaning gives way as swings do
When they leave still balance for air and reach.
Every return is a prayerful moment of inhale and exhale.
Children say, "Push me, push me",
And off into reach again,
The air answering unasked questions.
On return, only "Push me, push me"
As if understanding was meant to be found and lost
Repeating as the seasons do.

Mischief and melancholy

After reading that Plotinus was kind and humble
I understood why the One he discovered didn't impress
    the emperors...
All the emperors, BC and AD.
When I turned the corner with Levinas in my right hand
My metro card in my left I ran into a woman
Who asked me for a quarter.
I looked her in the eye and winked.
I handed her the book to free my hand for her quarter.
After a second I hauled out a quarter from my pocket.
When I handed it to her she wasn't there.
My book went with her.
Was it Levinas? Was it the price of the book?
I hadn't marked my place.
I was ready to dump Emmanuel and Plotinus,
Throw in my lot with the emperors.
In the grand scheme of life it doesn't take much
To learn the wrong lesson.

Ridiculous Man
(After Dostoevsky's short story)

Dostoevsky wakes from a dream.
He searched for a little girl whose cry for help
He had run headlong from
In a slow hobbled miserable conceit.
A sleep or two later,
Before and after....
Jesus shampoo bottled and sold:
Rinse and rinse again.
Crazy ridiculous entrepreneurial do-it-yourself
Sale's program for re-writing the gospels,
Bottling them. Liquid no more paradise
Than print or spoken word.

W.E.B.

In 1905 Dubois condemned Washington's 1896 speech:
You only have to look at five fingers to know
They are not all equally beloved by the palm,
Not even the wrist.

Takes time to look, to see, to turn up the heat.
After the water has boiled, burned a hole in the kettle,
And roils in the blood leaking out.

One soul, in the fiber of the intellect, slams his fist
Against deficiency, splintering all blocks and benches
Into nothingness, and starting over: Genesis
Of the world's ways and things.

One Giant Leap

When sapiens kept a giant step
It was into the same old mud
Rain stirs on the ground.
Private moon trips are an Epstein frontier
Always missing something, anything, anybody.
Adhesive
Dissolves
In a gummy mess
At the equator.

Perspective promised is myopia regained.
Just as lighted matches burn skin,
The way a plush Pullman car
Chugs into the knacker's yard.
Still good wishes sell as well as guns:
Have a good day can explode fractal distance.

When the moon softened sapiens footfall,
It had not rained for some time,
Shocking astronauts into a new perspective
On drought.

Perspective gained:
They understood
Analogy
As
Compassion.

Doubt Can Be A Problem

Doubt can be a problem
When it's your middle name.
Who calls their child "doubt"?

Humility got elected
But refused to take office.
Too small a margin.

Courage is something else,
Waking up knowing
What you went to bed knowing.

Patience like love on a mirror
Of shiny metal   can only wait
So long.

Prudence spoils, doubt festers,
Humility shrinks, courage is mobbed up
Cutting down forests.

Because the sky is nettled by branches,
Clouds are scratched by twigs, when children
climb they might see the face of god.

Flying Paper

Snow fell like origami
Breaking apart before landing.
Foolish to try to catch one,
Paper birds can't   be shot.

Peace trees flower origami reminders
Of atomic storms. Wise to pamper one.
The paper shivers, a child's breath
Blowing under its wings.

Teens at the border fly SOS on paper planes
Substituting for bottles. Guards drink beer
Out of cans which they crush in a single fist.
Then they wipe their mouths with paper litter.

Souls in the Lower Circles

A quiet hiding
    like the shiny white under the bark of the Plane tree
Beats taking a hiding.

Staying lost
    beats losing everything
The way wind whips the birch whose color is in its bark.

Shaving in the shower sans crystal
    beats facing yourself in a mirror
When a quiet hiding makes greater sense

Than dignity burning off like fat in a skillet.
    change is, after all, everybody's pseudonym
And Inquisition is a cancel reflex

We all have them
    reflexes,
Dunnage along the curbside of hell

BOOK III:
STICK OUT YOUR TONGUE

"To understand and judge a society, one has to penetrate its basic structure to the human bond upon which it is built... forms of labor, ways of loving, living, and dying."

(Maurice Merleau-Ponty)

Goons with Guns

Goons with guns glam up the ordinary
So it's the best place to hide...

Untangle laces
Get a haircut
Brush your teeth
Gargle salt water.

Don't invite strangers for pizza dinner
Don't drink rosé
Don't volunteer
Don't HOWL
Nor sing a song for yourself.

Don't drive a tank into town
Don't ask where the flowers are gone
Nor wonder out loud what Jesus
Would have to have said
To make much more of love?

Put a warm compress on your forehead
Get a haircut
Brush your teeth
Gargle with salt water.

Freedom's double E pops
The consonants into kneeling:
To repent? To implore?
To rearrange the letters
The way a swan turns.

Then a call "sh<u>oo</u>t" rings out:
Snake eyes? Double O license to kill.
The consonants stack up on the edge.
A leap from here can't be a metaphor.

Why not promise the bullies?
They can be free of their compulsion,
Ask the fat lady not to stop singing.

It's not all over until she can be fat and free
Brush your teeth
Gargle with salt water.

What would Jesus have had to say
To make much more of love.

There Are No Tanks

There are no tanks rolling down my street.
I imagine them and I'm looking for a place to hide.

If there were tanks and soldiers rolling
down my street, they would not be mine.

If the tanks and soldiers in them were mine
The tires would all get flats, the soldiers would sing.

If there were tanks and soldiers that were mine
I would give each one an aspirin.

I and all my neighbors would take an aspirin.
Each body's headache would be everybody's headache.

A second aspirin would evacuate us all
From my nightmare.

7/14/20

Like a stone fledged from a catapult
             wanting more
Like a rubber crowbar prying heat
             from the sun
Like spectacles broken underfoot by Marie Stopes
             to stem the reproduction of myopia

Like the bend of a tree
             reaching for light
Like the twist and turn of a boxer
             in a butterfly stroke
Like the strafed liver of a man executed today
             routed out of the circuitry of species singularity
Like Edison's legacy current throwing his limbs about
             his brain sucking air as if a jelly fish.

Oyez   Oyez   Oyez
A man executed for evil doing today in Indiana
             and all's well
The amygdala struts in uniformand high leather boots.
When they're off
These boots stand apart.
Oyez   Oyez   Oyez
And, all's well.

Some Things Have Changed (after Brecht)

On earth
    some things have changed
Is the letter I want to write
to émigrés friends on Mars:

"Some things have changed
on Earth now
Homeless now refers to people
with many homes.
No one is without a roof, a room
and a neighborly view.

The doors at the borders
have given way
to up and down escalators
moving
as they do.
Our sun's light
Like god's own eyes smiling
Spares the lungs of sapiens and pets
Pretty equally."

My letter will be one in a series
of lessons
to Mars:
Some things have changed
on Earth.

P.S. Some things have changed,
Turning-on-a-dime balance; better and worse still,
Moves toward checkmate.
Any advice from the Martians
Is welcome?

Stick Out Your Tongue

Stick out your tongue,
Break the circle of your face,
Take it off,
             Let it roll.
Lick the leaves,
             With your spittle.

The raging hairline of the forest,
Crowded like petulant children
             Sticking out their tongues.
It's in the genes.

Still when the door is ajar,
When the circle is broken,
The devil is on the run.

Think/Imagine

1. *"Gradually he came to understand that in the very
      impotence of his art
   there might be a miracle." (Katya Andreadakis/
   John Berger)*

2. A cardinal, full cassock, punches the air
   Sieg Heil and the rest.
   And I imagine Audubon shooting birds
   To take a close look.
   Purple red thread caught in trees
   Is easy to take down now
   The foliage is gone for the winter.

3. Eliot's "jew" sits on a cold windowsill,
   Unlike Rembrandt's Jewish Bride
   In the warmth of her father's hand.
   The name does what it's meant to do.
   Not Rembrandt's loving hand for sure.
   Maybe he had a Jewish friend: Spinoza?

4. If god bore Jesus he never meant
   Monotheism to strut its stuff.
   Which brings me to Jesus art.
   Paintings of him tend to show god's DNA
   Shining all about, even through great pain.

He's never looking you in the eye.
He's watching to be looked at.
He pulls a hair from his eye.
To blow it off as heresy.
Watch him share bread
Like there's no tomorrow.
That's why we resurrect him
With incendiary determination.

5. If Adam had a Q-tip,
    He might have heard the serpent snarl
    Stomped him into the dust
    Or become a mother, not Eve.
    Labor would have a different meaning
    Like the curl of a wave in the sand
    Can make music and a truck load of debris.
    A Q-tip. How strange is that?

6. Think of a hairy laid-back old tree
    With "Posted" on its belly.
    Imagine it's ambition in its curls and waves.

    Think of the dark coming in early.
    Imagine the knuckles of a cold wind.
    Think about limping on a stubbed toe.

    Imagine the old tree patting its belly.
    Think about the logic of symbolic forms,
    What it might say a virus is.
    Or in the theology of sapiens dominion
    Imagine how many people in one place
    Tweeting alleluia or lackaday, god might need
    To recognize a righteous one.

7. Damson taste is not for everyone
   It's a purple fruit
            all the way from China.

   "In Sodom 10 righteous neighbors
   Would have saved them all,
   The angel tells Jacob."

   Sweaty and swarthy Jacob demanded:
   "Bless me. Bless me!"

8. Still in earshot the angel whispered:
   "Try living like one of the 10."

   Jacob unrelenting: "If I had hope
   I would open my hand. Still I listen
   For a serenade at the keyhole."

Simone Weil Wrote

Simone Weil wrote: so long as we are in struggle
Against evil, each bit of evil we destroy grows up
Again as before.

Ouch!
Splat!

Can one, a person I mean, be a saint
And live past thirty-three?
Can a person live to thirty-five
Without an ego?
Can a person check ego at the bar
And survive a gunfight?

Boom!
Bam!

Could it be we see underbrush bramble
Broken branches entangled vines
Throttled thistle as detritus of war
To be avenged?
Like police officers afraid of their own
Hands and feet.
In the woods, surrounding houses
Can be friends and cousins
Because 500 year old trees can be saints.

Oorah!
Amen!

Roots

(one impulse for a vernal wood)

This wood would not rot.
It would not.
I didn't want to trip
Nor break my hip
      (at my age).
But it would not rot.

I took a can of blue paint,
A thick bristled brush,
Daubed the root line
To effect a reminder, a landmark,
A reminder that what doesn't rot
Is what we've got, to make our way,
A bridge to imagine on.

Before you bang your head
On the floor pile up some pillows.
Either way you bounce, padding helps.
Stand on them if you prefer,
Gain height   like Everest. Depends only
On what's counted and who counts.
Then again, losing height is an option
Like ice caps melting, watch out
For your carbon tread, intemperate
It will make you trip.
      oh that hip).

Humanity on Trial

In the days before and after,
Leather straps against palms sculpt meaning.
Callouses are natural healers, but rough.

It all takes place on the sidewalk
Of immediacy, when poetry loses its song,
When schismatics are clowns and bullies
The archangel of longing beckons.

After Velcro tying laces is for chimps.
Look at the evidence:
Chewable vitamin C
Wet nurses of all sorts.
Elon Musk announces:
If it takes a coup we do a coup.

We didn't create the world. But living
One day in seven is no garden.
A twist of bark gives the tree
The look of a spinning top,
a dubious gift that is ever flummoxing.

Hemmed for the duration of the trial
Baggy pants give the wrong impression
(Or the right one according to the wrong people)
Of grown-ups shitting themselves.
So tough to feel small
And want to feel like god.

For the defense: the warm garden was a ruse.
The button maker needs coats and shirts,
Frocks and sweaters. There had to be clothes.
It was all a set up.

Thread is fraying
Where to put the longing?
Not in a museum,
Not in a safety deposit box.
Compassion fossilizes so quickly.

Golems are all those Noah denied.
Ghosts live on, sip energy through straws.
Turns for the worst are like ground hammered by horses.
Turns for the better return in sentences and glyphs.
Genesis all over again, and all over again.
A record of sorts.

Unless and Until

Love
        In a hammock
close to the ground,
Coccyx bruising coming.

Any container for love
        grinds it.
The way herbicides grow flowers
and kill the roots.

The rug merchant invites you to kneel
        to test the magic.
He will tell you the loose thread in the corner
is to remind that only god is perfect.

Truth is
        the flaw is a human mistake.
Best just follow the signs,
the exits are all numbered.

Love allowed
        permitted to wander and land
will try to befriend ideas of good behavior
until
        until
the rain wets the slide.

Slippery and devoted at the OK corral
        at dawn
                at sunset.
What else?

Unless
        unless
it's love that pricks
the conscience of the king?

Big Bang/Big Question

What is life with your back to the sun?

When the music stops people will trip over each other
for a beach chair.

Without doubt hope is a mystery.

Put a slab on a spit at the pool,
char it alongside tomatoes.
See, there is some good in everything.

Even empires on the edge of dementia,
stockpiling broken toenails and camel manure.

If each person's microbiome is different,
a hundred trillion microbes of difference,
how do we all get along before they do?

Country Club Bigots

She's in my arms on the bed.
Excited birds outside, soft porn spectators.
Their whistle on the street
would be offensive.
Their pecking on wood by a neighbor
would be intrusive.
The odd one crashing into the glass
could be just dessert.
Sirens declare it's noon.
Other sirens register uncertain lives.
The radio, which we forgot to turn off,
reports from the Mexican border and Gaza.
I imagine myself on a South Hampton beach.
Very soon, anxious, the country club bigots
might be off their leashes.
Then I feel her fingers in my eyebrows
which curl quickly and I'm thinking'
perhaps the bigots are lying on beds,
excited as birds. Glad to be in a quiet hotel room.

Playtime

Scrabblers play:
"Confederate" is worth 75 points in the right position.
"Y" gives "Yankee" its value, should be on the flag

flying high over a bloated house
in which breathers believe others
owe them air.

The piano is dumped like a machine
no longer able to detect scratching
or warps in the stairs to the stars.

The end was always in the pedal note
and the pitch.

Kept In

There's a painting in the Fennimore Cooper House
(in Cooperstown) of a black schoolgirl
in a pinafore dress.

She's on a school bench, stretching backwards
in a relaxed pose. Her pigtails cupped in her palms,
fingers at rest in each other.

She's not relaxed. She's dressed in pretty garments,
but her socks are worn to thread
and her shoes dusty.

Her feet are raised at the heel,
her toes almost on point.
A book sprawled on the floor at her side.

I read the title, "Kept In."
So this is punishment and this is resilience
1889, oil on canvas.

Common Good

The river that runs through cracks in the heart.
The waterfall that washes away gratitude.
The grass that grows under your feet.
The rain that spits out methane against its will.
The fear that mocks and mimics at the same time.
The scavenger brain that thrives on decay.
The cry that cracks underfoot like a neck.
The words that lie on the lips.
The horns of dilemma.
The words that moisten like vaseline.
The cedar that keeps moths out of the bedclothes.
The music in the landing gear of dry leaves.

We took a fall when the worm turned in Eden.

Protest Near a Catskill Cemetery

Swagged up
        golf pants
        unmatched socks
a stolen police baton in one hand
in the other his fragile grip.

In a crowd screeching chicken at him.
His tense fingers stretched out
        like skin
        on a scarecrow.
His blood letting into gutters
with other unremembered people
        and unnamed warriors.
Some reciting Chaucer in Olde English.
Some Dante in Italian.
Some speeches of Nelson Mandela in Xhosa.

In a corner of the cemetery he sees
Stars of David, the underground railroad
must have dropped Jews off here at times.
Potato farms and field hand homes are gone
        and churches...
You can still hear horns playing
        like Louis Armstrong
Singing in doppelganger voices
        of Marian Anderson and
        Billie Holiday.

Tyranny Redux

I see snow geese and mandarin ducks
adapt...
They fly less and eat sparingly.

Humans are molting
now,
Since haircuts are illegal.

Eva Braun's knickers went for $5k
at auction.
Adaptation is a miracle.

Walking Backwards

Dorothy Parker and MLK
(Excuse my dust, sir)
She sent him beloved forget-me-nots
Invisibly attached to the moon
In a perennially waxing mode.

But no, that's not the real moon.
Ms. Parker and Dr. King are dead.
Ashes to ashes while the Supremes sing
Out of tune: the fire this time.

Still, rivers are damp and gas smells awful
(We might as well live)

Addicted

Sinkholes are depressions
Unresponsive to meds.

Suicide will go up when war,
Academics, and crime are as dormant as Etna.

Seatbelts required open up the imaginations
For self-murder.

Mass suicide is an insurmountable persuasion
When sugar-rotten teeth are replaced with asbestos, lead,
    and opioid falsies.

Eat drink and look for the ferryman
To bring you across.

Or fire his ass, and to quote my friend Ping Ferry:
Don't let the bastards get away with it.

BOOK IV:
PHEW!

Phew!

Phew!
Zino–like I didn't expect to get there.
Phew!
Anyway, catching yourself holding your breath
Lets you take your fist out of your pocket,
Open your hand. Wet a finger,
Hold it to the wind.
Phew!
Getting there may be a fruitless ambition,
There is fruit on the way, and that kiss
The one that knocked Juliet's socks off,
The one so misunderstood of Judas.
Phew!
You could have heard Barabbas cop the plea.

Poem For Another Day

A queue is a kind of together
Just after and before separate
A kind of separate
Until the next day and the next bus.

Of an evening...
The question I ask myself
Is why the riddle
Read R. D. Laing again.
Civilization and Discontents
Looked for cues in liberation theology
Not so far.
We still come in with tooth and claw armor
Read Reich again
Read Marx again
Cues?
Not so far.
Suffering still sprays like skunk spit
Blue in the blood, Dracula
Read Mary W. again
Read the bible again
Clues?
Not so far
Not this evening.

Of an evening I get to wonder
What we do and what we do.
Thoughts like cellophane noodles
Leave a body hungry and exposed.
A threadbare sinner in an iron mask,
Read Dumas again
For clues.
Gasping wide mouthed sucking
On sweat and metal
Try to wipe your lenses with shirt tails
Wipe to see to wipe to see   what you can...
To solve the riddle
Together.   to solve the riddle of an evening.
To queue together to solve the riddle.
Sanctify the queue
Let it be a convivial place.

It's been said pain can be seen in every
Blade of grass, you can see it growing.
With so much agony, why not take a break
From human sacrifice, the damage we do
To each other. There will be enough
Suffering without ours.

My feet are damp
From walking on water.
But that's a poem for another day.

Mystery of Love

Reveille to taps
to reveille
always getting back up.
Blow your horn Gabriel
open the pearly gates
at the border
of disorder.
Bring in the family,
bring in the missus
and the kids.
Reveille   walls have to have doors
windows,
tap on the window
watch it turn to sand
with footprints of escape
and arrival.
Blow your horn Gabriel
LOUD.
Okay to whimper on the inhale,
press your lips
to blow a kiss
wet with the holy mystery of love.

Stranger with a Familiar Face

Cymbeline's mom wanted his head bashed in
bleeding thin
as python's spittle.
His glory, her glory, her choice
his end of dreams, naked
a doll with pins in it.

When she peeled artichokes
she didn't cry.
When she peeled onions she did.
Except when she needed just a little
for flavoring.

Howl, howl at the mother who promises
her child, the son, the father whose children
want the moon.
A child's fantasy   sick metaphor
naked as kids bathing
each bobbing a doll under water.

Pray not to be prey, importunate embrace.
Pray, why don't we, to learn
from the opposite of what we want.
Lie down with wisdom
a stranger with a familiar face.

Lord Nelson

At the end of the movie, Mrs. Hamilton
Korda's Nelson, one arm, one eye,
dying asks Hardy, his #2,
to kiss him on the way out.
Raymond Chandler might have Marlowe summarize:
Kiss tomorrow good-bye.

So ambiguous   ambivalent   ambidextrous
kiss of death   kiss him off
could kiss her, so kind, so kind.
What's left after I've kissed you all over
and you tell me to kiss your ass?

And then, there's the kiss of life.
Could that be what Nelson was thinking?

Shape of the World

The shape of the world is not quite
the shape the world is in.
That being said, who really knows.

On the internet photo-shopping for a dog
with a horn like a unicorn,
the kind of growth on your foot that hurts,
bunion which sent John running
for a pilgrim's progress.

Reach out a hand to a mezuzah.
Kiss a couple of fingers to touch it,
not OCD, close listening for a repetition of love.
Not unlike mistletoe   which evacuates two people
at the same time from thinking about their feet.

The shape of the world is not what it feels like
to stand on it, thinking about the Ghastly Future,
Paul Erlich's repeat performance in 2020:
Not wrong   not wrong   not wrong
which is to say not not being, not being outside
the footing of being thrown off one's gait
and closing a chapter.

Hoody

(Listening to a witness makes the listener a witness. —Elie Wiesel)

Of late I like to wear hoodies.
Let the policemen look.
Let him find a jew,
mongrel warrior carrying a wreath
to the tomb of the unknown bastard.
Poor bastard!
I didn't resist arrest, I kissed him
the way Dostoevsky's Jesus kissed
his Father policeman.
Let him repent
with me. Entrapped is worse than doubt.
Not too late to salvage each of us.

So Long a Border

Along   a long the border
crucifix in hand
lips on the savior's feet at every trip
and fall, moving stealthily like a slow
freight train sliding through the Middle Passage
as if looking for a match
to burn up a baby in a basket, in a basket
floating along the Mason-Dixon line
to a tango of witches.

He came in uniform, sleeves rolled.
He grasped the baby. She kissed a wisp of hair
blown in the tussle. He kissed the baby too:
Why am I doing this? He doesn't know.
He arrives home late, kisses his own sleeping child.
The lady in the lake, still a girl, promises him comeuppance.
He believes her.

The woman at the border finds his home.
She abides in the bulrushes of his pond.
She hears the smack of widowhood
and fatherlessness.

Macadam

When immigrants arrive somewhere safe
they kiss the earth, even macadam.
Somewhere
is the air wanderers breathe.
Wherever they land is always a somewhere
that could look like where they are from
before they can get up off their knees.
Paved fields are mirrors of their souls
broken and rebuilt for working purposes.

Observers say tyrannies are inevitable:
Desperation makes desperadoes of us all.
Going along is the icepack of exhausted reaching.
Melting is inevitable. Water is the liquid of melancholy,
the juice of eros, the milkweed of honeybunch,
the tears of the luck of the draw, the embrace of grace
or the toxic brew of broken glass and rusty nails.

Elect to break the ice!
Elect to break the ice!
asap

Elements of Striving

Oh, yes
love it....
salami slices before
iterations of emporia
came and went

Oh, yes
love it...
archeologists have found 50-million-year-old
male insects with genitals intact.
Who knew insects had balls?

No hint of a cross
in the snow dust signals at the digs.

Oh, yes
love it...
ein sof
fullness of gratitude
amplitude
chocolate dripping from the thumbs of children.

Oh, yes
love it...
cookies hot off...
like a kiss to passing children
before iterations of emporia
came and went
filaments of striving
no record at the digs.
But who knew
shopkeepers have balls?

Keeping Warm

There's coal under the snow.
In the fire we're burning wood.
My hands are black
digging
just taking advantage of what's near:
twigs   coal   deer pellets
nauseating smell
like a stifled kiss caught
on the inside of dry lips
quartered by second thoughts
which comes out in discharge
as from a wound.
What I wanted was warm blood,
the kind that runs in the veins of gods
and other immortals.

Schism

Begin this story with the way it ends.
And we see subheads indicating 1 hour ago, 3 months
    earlier,
And the child going backwards, the film is rewinding to
    show her entering.

The story ends with a pair of twins taking a bath,
The hue of each in the other's feathers.
Only one is in the water, splashing. The second is the one
About to get in once she is no longer moving backwards.

Taking Off

(As the comic strip tells it, Superman's parents rocketed him from home to save him from Kryptonite catastrophe)

Your father is older than most children's fathers, his mother told him. He remembered her telling him that as if it was the first thing she said to him ever. He never could think about her without remembering that his father was older than most children's fathers. She told him that very soon after he was born, and she told him it many times afterward too. Some nights soon after he was born he remembered hearing her telling his father how much older he was than most young children's fathers. He heard her saying that while she tucked up father and kissed him goodnight. She tucked father up like she tucked him up. Soon after he was born he noticed her tucking father up. He watched her tucking father up as he waited for her to come to him. Dad was tucked up first then she tucked him up. He didn't like waiting. He told mother he didn't like waiting. Soon after he was born he wanted her to know he didn't like waiting. As soon as he could talk he told mother he didn't like dad being tucked up first. After mother tucked him up she went back to father. He could hear them talk. He could hear mother tell dad how son wanted to be tucked up first. He wanted to tell her not to tell dad. He wished dad did not know about his wanting to be tucked up first.

Balance

It was like the trial of god
when my father danced. I never
believed he could, and he could.
Every celebration he would move
effortlessly readying himself for soft shoe triumph.
(Looked to me like he would fall)
Melting prayers in my head.
I was not a believer. He knew about balance.

What is a Good Story
(After Costa Gravas' "Betrayed")

Farmer Tom gets his mail on Friday.
Brings home the bacon.
Leads his family in grace
Before meals. Puts his feet up,
After kissing his wife
For a great meal.

Out back his pets are fed
Before bed. Also, the man held
For the hunt on the sabbath.
The chase comes and goes. Blood
Is spilled, some color on his pants
Not noticed.

Tom gets his mail on Monday.
As always in the winter the mailbox snaps
To release a letter or two and lots
Of supermarket discount coupons.
Along the putted driveway windchimes
Knock on heaven's door, a stone winged angel
Is silent in meditation, cracks on the road
Grin at the ensemble. Rope thread and spent bullets
Dismembered litter in a surreal gallery hidden
By the unseeable the dogs are still chewing on.

If not slaves   hostages.

x

What is a story
About what makes no sense
But a leaf praying for water
Betwcen mountains and melts
Moistening deep french kisses.

What is spring
But a surprise of strangers
                    as is
                    as is
                    is....
What is spring after all
But terror flushed out
In the profoundest crying.
What is a good story
But the profoundest crying
No longer slave,
Now hostage.

East/West

Cross-legged yoga   pose
Can feel like the 4 by 8 of the cross
Not the tree of life.

Tree   pose maybe   8 by 16
Knowledge of good and evil
Will weary your one leg.

Undisputed   turns
Of events are how the news
Reports the news. Used to be
History repeats itself

Like long and short form
Tai Chi. The smell of power
In another room is an undisputed
Putrid more pungent than a skunk's
Squirt.

Give the tyrant five ripe tomatoes
Watch Kiss of the Spider Woman serialized,
The smell of artificial intelligence
Will be thick in the air for as long
As your members take to repair
(Remember).

Yellow-Livered

Pictured at the bar tell:
totems burned in the fractal plains,
covenants clawed out of gin bottles
fisted on opposing sides.

Oil clogs up burial grounds,
madams kiss regulars,
Jim Crow's arthritis flares up
Along with his holster
on Jill Crow's lap. Wizards
alchemize cures, voodoo
Looks enlightened.

All this over thin strands of hair
Samson sensibility, only destruction
satisfies. Liver transplants cure
yellow tint. Everyone at the bar
has someone's else's liver.
No one drinks. Bourbon yellows
like Dorian Gray back in
the day.

Gratitude bubbles in orange juice
and soda. A large man drops one foot
Over a child's footprint along a snow boundary
He wipes his eyes.
It only seems pointless.
He drops the other foot inside an adult's
Bigger than he is. Wet penetrates
The patches on his shoes, ecru credit cards
Spill out of his vest pocket.

Everyone here needs a new liver.
rumor is burial grounds are where
the liver is mined. Anyway
they toast together every Friday
night tight in orange juice and soda:
> *Thank the good lord*
> *Any liver in these parts*
> *Works for anybody*
> *From around here.*

Three Fifths

Simplify   complexify   (a rare word
Just heard).

All men (an historic term for sapiens)
Are created equal.
All sapiens?
Except....

Accept
it
objects are not sapiens.
Who is not what.
What is not who.
Except....

What can't be schizophrenic.
Simplify and complexify,
Two is one is who.
Accept
it

Three fifths is a fraction of what.
Except....

What is to infinity
As who is to nothing
If nothing is the eternity of the soul.
Not bare feet on a barge
rotting in the haze
of who to who combat.
Sweat soaking the pitch
tossing ballast overboard
Old sport   old son
                    boy.

Being is never something
Always something else
Except....
Me real   you shadow
Three fifths casts a different shadow.

Accept
it
that's something else.

                    x

Could be a mathematical crux
of nature, holy numerals
in defined sequence and finitude:
three fifths
the number Ham drew in his oh so careful
retreat,
the number Delilah grabbed at the deli counter
kept her in line for days.

Van Gogh's peasants bent to labor
can look like the fraction
of personhood
God painted, by color at first
before the flood, indelibly
nothing came out in the wash.

Think time, think duration
kisses tainted by dye
burned through time like lye
on bedlinen,
giving the lie
to "all" in sapiens etc. etc.

It was a surprise to learn elephants
have feeling   memory   dolphins love and kiss
cause and effect,
simple and complex

x

Cannibalism is a secret ubiquity.
To save the rainforest
stop building auction blocks
three fifths of every platoon dies in battle.
Survivors scratch at phantom fingers
three at a time.
Humanism is never sufficiently human
mistakes quiddity for meat and manhood.

Ice on the roof freezes quickly,
faster than the sun rises to the task of melting
history.
All in a week's work
the world gets bigger as it shrinks
three fifths, and then it's the weekend.
Unless the sabbath is a secret.
No surprise the world must shrink
with every inch of growth.

Inquisition   execution   pyres   and crematoria
will do that.
Every leap in population means an equal
and opposite   fraction recalibration
of the norm:
three fifths
mouths wide open
not for dental repair
not for identification by molar
just for surprise…

Duration is a doozy
in the pale
        vale
        of
        settled
in a spasm of muscle and bone
simply stressed
complex construction
of what is real
        who?

x

The compass and the clock are the faces
sapiens has grown accountable to.
the impossibility of turning back the hands
without reference to the colors in nature
        seasonal shades
        and plays of light.

Four corners of a table
legs of a chair
stand on equal footing.
shades longer, less glued, dove and broken tail,
butt deflated just like
the rounded head of one bone
sitting in the cup of another.

Five fifths.
No compromise
if the desk is to be written on
if the chair is to be sat on.

                x

The voice said: build a boat
storm ahead   a big one.
You'll need 5 decks
each one the ceiling of another.
The lower decks will be hotter
less air, everybody   every animal
save your family and pets
go below, fed and bed in the three lowest
decks, call that below decks.

You'll be the first to see my dove
and you'll call those below decks *workers*.
They will rebuild after 40 days and 40 nights.
I picked you for your high-level executive function.
Now's the time to make amends.
Seven days up front was not enough.
Time to get the show on the road again.

Except reason
Wrests on a greasy scaffold.

Accept
it

will try to conform to the dial
of the time.

Hand to Mouth

The globe before discovery
Was a balloon, boundary-less
before it became a toy
with a light in it.

A child's fingerprint shone
a thumb on The Congo, a pinkie
on New Orleans, Jefferson's deal
with Napoleon.

Leopold's chocolate kingdom took
tears to melt, hand to mouth;
catch and hatch concerti
in all his salons.

Womb production, no kisses
came before factories   heartbreak and civil war,
interstate commerce, world trade, keep the blankets
on the bed. Nite Lite to the potty for a while.
Then stronger wattage to read adventures by,
and Mr. Rogers stories.
As on any farm the stakes are inexorably
pummeled in.

Sophia

I like to kiss her neck
                four times
points of the compass
lines of the cross
                the seasons.

I see you Sophia
a baby kissing her mother's neck,
a child having it away with Barbie,
a teenager in love with someone
                like Ken.

I like to kiss her neck
                four times
for each of her passions
                before me
                for me.

                                        x

At one time she played with books
                upside down
                inside out.
What was believed in her house
was bone marrow embedded in cave
stone
                etherized

on tablets wrest from mountains
marked, *return to sende*r
Time was a bed of nails
Was thought to secure a quiet night
Or two of thought. Many believed
They could run dry between rain drops
(Which as children millions believed possible.)

Her father called the mare Sophia
                          too.
Rode her singing Irish shanties
                          melodic
then there's a kick in the butt
                          but
what they believed was the matter.

x

Entropic?
Does wisdom fade?
Can it relate to any misadventure?
Can it feel pain?
Will it regrow forest
            after fire?
Is flood her ever-ready sidekick?
Is she susceptible to kissing?
Will she become involved with me
            when the rivers divide?

The genes and gems of sapiens
will wander   up the wrong tree bark
to lament the tree
to forget the tree.

She lets me go in the water
        all over again,
original sin: Not to be born again
        not my choice
out on a limb
        limbic lassitude
in the bark

x

She jokes. Has me in stitches.
My debt finds an alloy.
The stallion stalks Sophia.
The price of a thoroughbred is beyond rubies.
        sand moves...
Scrunch up your flag
        in the frosty air.
        Sedimentally filled
        full of....

The word in Sophia's ear is no sound
        empty bellows.
There is a myth in the wind
telling of Sophia's kissing a chap
who abandoned her.

She caught up with him
looking like a stag.
The chap could not resist.
She once burned quickly   played dead.
Better than being killed.

Sophia from the ground sees me.
Kisses me four times
on the neck.
Wipes the slate.
I rise like a calf
scampering away from the field of battle
at birth.

Survivors

Before
the day
    was over
berkait
    linked
    barbed
spitting
    blood
licking
    the finger
washing out
    the mouth.

Vehamatav
    no appetite
    for
    blood
a blessing
    no
    disguise

Tal vaz
    maybe
crossing
the street

won't
require
help
    maybe
the paving
    moves

    why
    in
    hell
    not?

Night
falls
    first
    on
    children.
They sleep
    through it
    except
    to pee.
When it falls
    on moms
    and dads
as it does
    at
    night
everybody
    pees
    wets
    themselves.

Long since
   en-
   slaved
her dentures
   like fingerprints
make her
   as her.
For her husband
         cooking
         with gas
         is prohibited,
fumes in concentrated
         plumes
         scorch
even basements.

Should I say more?
         why not?
Battering rams do a job
boring can crack
         a skull
daylight
         burns...
a blind grandfather
         can only
         feel it.
Hasn't seen the moon
         for years
         before
         capture.
Should I say more?
         why not?

Handel did:

    Comfort ye
behind closed doors
    maybe
Tal vaz
The old blind man sang
      as he walked
      under his breath.
Singing was like a wisp
     of a kiss
     into thin air
     like a hungry balloon
     taking in
     helium.

Merde alors

            lost
            in
            conflation

the way
   shit
   happens

Kyssas
   freeze
   overnight,
the great kiss off
between
ask and you shall find
and in neither
   ask
   nor tell.

Udugu

        will

        power

crocs have their own woke

on the horizon.

Not a joke.

        waters rise

        with sunshine.

                rain

                bows

        loose their arrows.

Rakhana

        salt

        in

        the wound.

Walk half blind

        in tears

for the murdered.

Turning Point

In the blue corner
is Hippocrates weaving.
In the red, hypocrisy
bouncing and bopping
up and down.
Meant to be exits
the corners are comfort zones.
Corner men are toweling their guys.
In the blue the challenger's team
feigns confidence.
In the white corners it's snowing
so the boxers can swish and spit.
Butterfly and bee weave and bounce
across the square. The count

           the count

           the count

by the clock, tipping point
like an umpire's holy kiss
is ephemeral.

Looking For Our Equal

I shovel snow, send up spray.
My tires combust mounds
as if lake effect was a craft,
as if trees shuffling off snowflakes
imitated human engineering.

Religious impulse is elemental.
We are gods looking for our equal
as if pi recorded the logic of trust,
as if venn presented all the ways shame
brings blood to the eyes of angels
snogging on a pin.

The Body Politic

Bone marrow
Will deploy squads
To eviscerate not self-invaders.
Thymus more circumspect
Will try to turn enemies into friends.
Don't blame the marrow
Nor heap great praise on the thymus.
What it takes for safety may be felled
Like the walls of Jericho, by desire
Mounted on what looks like a safe bet.
A catch, under divine mistletoe.

Hope

She with hope in her teeth,
as I think John Berger imagined her,
can't help it: she bites through french kisses.
She rejects politesse.
She has to mean it.
That's what hope measures:
How much you mean it.

The Reproduction of Shame

Hangs between both their legs,
legacy of broken trust,
backpacks full to overflowing
                          with fear,
fear of what and why
I am, you are.

Like a rose by any other name
the kisses of life are thorny,
you only have to google to know
                          more.
Something about wanting
                          something
imagined. By all means
by other means
                          than expected.

Sound and Light Frequencies

1

Let there be light
   and there was dark.
Let there be food
   and there was greed.
Let there be hunting
   and there was murder.

After ill-gotten kisses,
the barn door was closed
with ten long tablets
prone to cracking
   under pressure.

2

The way Buddha's right and left eye
held perforated pitch.
Gone to be the Buddha.
Wife and child, eyes and lips
unfold through sound
and light frequencies.

3

The last to come home
prodigal   embrace

The last back
brings the grist of remembering;
and the risk.

Every fingernail takes
when it grows
The scratch every itch longs for.

Carcass

(After Charles Baudelaire's "Fleurs du Mal")

An imagined reminiscence
unlike the man in the moon
unlike Lenin's face in the snow;
maybe edible
like a peach among vegetables
if not crushed,
or albumen guarded well against yolk.

Imagine Baudelaire's lover boiling up
like a dancer leaping off a trivet
somehow overheated by his "je ne sais quoi."
Maybe
irascible "quoi"
telling her she will soon be kissing worms,
"qui vous mangera de baisers"
when her image in his mind is a messy sketch.

Could have been different.
Could not have been at all.
Lenin in the snow, why not?
Man in the moon, ask Elon or Jeff.
Lady lover kicking up worms
while the poet picks losses from his scalp
as any carcass.
Maybe edible
like guacamole coughing up unripe avocado
or merlot packing toenails.

Same Old Same Old

There are ghosts
in old houses,
in new houses
on old foundations.

There are ghosts
who whisper, cajole,
seduce, pat, kiss, smack,
spit, leave.
Return is something else again.

There are ghosts
with broken necks
and bullet holes,
a finger might pick out
the slime bred in them.

Some ghosts are angels
with contrition in their wings.
Respect and forgive
worn like socks.
They don't spit.
Everything else is ditto,
another house on old foundations.

Bun and Burger

A head cold is a euphemism
for cold feet,
afraid to say into the mirror
I don't care about that this and the other.
What I care about is trivial,
like untying a knot without cutting the cord.

A sprained foot, notorious since Achilles,
is to explain not taking a stand,
afraid to say into the mirror
I don't want to, I don't wish him harm,
I don't care if he kisses my sister.
No fight, no foul.

Like the starving starling sang:
I'd sell the world for a burger
if I'm honest.
You can burn the bun
for all I care.

Imagine You are Coached by an Angel.

He wears white shirt orange pants
A syringe in his top pocket
Where a red hankie would suit.

A daughter bears a child.
Love can co-habit with longing
The way sweat can smell sweet.

Imagine you are coached by an angel

From Dominica, he lays tile, warns:
Never trash a man who collects trash for a living,
Never pillage promises made to children.

Tin will slice a finger, a tongue.
Beware canned kisses,
Words double as sticks and stones.

Imagine you are coached by an angel

Fossils reveal shame is the sand trust trysts on.
A woman opens her raincoat to a man
He gives her bus fare. Her words pop pop

In his head like a shaken soda bottle.
Bring a change of clothes for a downpour.
A can of sardines, brain food, for a snack.

Imagine you are coached by an angel.

Beware of crowds, boots stomp on people's feet
Like netted crabs forced to smell each other's blood.
That's when they bite.

All Is Well

My grandfather
    touched his stick
to the ground
    lightly
    smiled
into his shoulders
    grateful
for the arm   he leaned on
to cross
    the street
    blind
since he turned
    forty or forty-one.

He asked few questions
    inquisition
cancel reflex
    he didn't share.

Beethoven could hear better deaf
    he said
Straightened the yarmulke on his head
Blake had a red-green problem
    touched his stick

Lloyds   *you have to*
            laugh
Insurance   *against loss?*
            you have to laugh.

x

Pope Francis sounds
like Rodney King:
why can't we get along?

On a stele
        on the landslide
        side of a hill
Hammurabi's code
        stands
        erect
as any purple pill
        for photographs
of mourners knelt
        at cenotaphs.

x

You (and I) read Žižek
We (and I) recall:
        Dostoevsky's
Jailer   Kiss å kiss
             with Christ,

Imagining   beyond
            profit

                    ground
                    cover
for deer shit
where pebbles were cleared for
                              carrots.
We (he) know about   the petty
                      freedoms
                      of honest work:
reality of load
            real of wind
            in the garret
No!
            he quotes
            he quotes
                    from the logo
over a concentration camp:

Work
      Sets
            Us
                  Free
(albeit he regrets
            the source)
Oh oh Žižekky

                              x

Children of a certain age will titter
            at
            briefs
And knickers
      on the line

after   the first burial
is the unconscious
the wind has undies nuzzle,
for a moment
     then all
     of a flutter.

Like his hands
          under her skirt
her fingers turn off the lights
         his got burned
under the lampshade.

She puts a mylar blanket
        around her,
        crushes the bulbs
under foot
        cuts
        the current
           off
           off.

                 x

My mother said
        he had the constitution
of an ox
        the navvy
        now dead
I spoke to of a morning
on the line outside my window
before train time
      while I put on socks.

My mother also said he was a prince
      (of a man).
She only saw him swing
         his hammer
         once.
She surmised
         the way the UK constitution
is reprised.
In the US it's on browning paper
         frayed
the way debt
can be   defrayed.

                x

A screech will not staunch
            Bleeding.
A rubric won't
         bow
to healing.

When a mouse   runs
       swoosh
You're seeing   satan

          craven
          chasing
hungry for the chaste.

                x

Nothing is   without
         pseudonym:

Old nick   nom de
                 guerre

all is well.

Natural Allies

They fondle in the bush
at the end of the drive
next to our anorexic birch,
the one with a squirrel shape attached
to make you think
                the birch has hidden talent.

The steering wheel sticks in the arch
of his back. Her hands hold his waist
as if she's driving. The gas runs out
                in flame.
They throw coffee cups and pizza ends
into the bush,
                shadows of more unmoored
                specter of uncaptained loins.

He turns   prayerful look on him.
She turns   away
to steady her pedestal.
Natural allies, soul mates.

Send in the doves...
You can hear the cooing
                in the under   growth,
fuse wire back to the original cry.

In a light wind the rope on the flagpole
rings an "I'm so sorry"   moan:
"the breaks failed."
In a strong wind the sound is fierce:
"no do over   no do over."

Bring in the nephrologists
There's an elimination problem
                    here.

In the light wind
"why not?   why not
                    let Hochmah be free
She is no winebibber
                    she is convivial."

BOOK V:
WHAT IS HIDDEN
AND HIDDEN FROM

Convention

A bunch of men
        who would have passed by
My grandfather, my father—

A bunch of men
        who hired mercenaries
To enshrine slavery
The way Magna Carta
        locked in monarchy.

A bunch of men
        who inseminated with their own semen
Other sapiens
        to cover debt.

A bunch of words
        each letter limping to higher purpose
Strung sentences in a line
        to catch the sun.

A bunch of words
        tanned
To find comity
        with those born sunburned
A bunch of rights grew
A bouquet in the red soil
        of new beginnings

As if an indoor outdoor rug
   in a slaughterhouse.

A bouquet of Rights
   stunning like dahlias and wisteria
Grown on rocks
Roses lilies mums on cracked sand.

The Hitch

1. The hitch in the evolution of thought is taut
    On a wire barb tearing at the logic of magic
    And the magic of logic.

    Indifferent to the yellow nail I've grown
    I am unmoved by those who limp, and those
    Whose ankles crack like dry twigs.
    I deflect by looking at my other foot.

2. News alert: nuclear bombs are plentiful
    As bruised apples. Oh ye orchards and garden
    Behold Cain   and Cain again!

    The pollinator rhymes in mysterious ways.
    Pinch on the bum recalls back when a slice
    Of a prisoner's buttock was a fried delicacy
    Among the denizens of war.

3. Think of Handel's Messiah sung by colonists:
    "and we will be made indestructible   indestructible."
    And sing into the night, and a change in the weather.

    I just heard Dr. King's 'friends and countrymen'
    speech
    With all the tears and rattle of a promissory note,
    The one when young people refuse to limbo:
       "Make all the rough places plain."

4. Like barbed wire holly survives lost generations
   Of ilex. I hate barbed wire. Chasing the devil's tail
   To draw blood.

   When leaves have a certain deterrent value.
   Even wasps turn away, instead sting children
   In the grass, playing where dandelions shake their
   shoulders
   And make grown-ups pee.

5. Such is teleology's gossamer spin, the transmission
   Of impulses along nerves, how sound waves travel,
   Or while roasting marshmallows
   How HHthe heat rises through the rod

   Into my hand. And the way moral fiber loses its spunk:
   Sapling certainty gives way to oak root rectitude,
   And cobweb attitudes screw with each other.

The Way We R

The morning's colors are today's.
Other days like this have libraries
Of poets and portraits kneeling in awe.
So it's all been seen before;

Yet not like this, these are today's colors

South Carolina just passed a death penalty bill:
Firing squads to replace drugs, Gunmen ride again.
37 cons will kick the can. Yesterday is today.
Yet not like this;

Going back goes beyond repeat.

The echoes of anonymity are in the air
It matters who is welcome.
Winds flare, snow drift chaos looks like heaven
To some because it is reliably white.

It doesn't take an abacus.

Granite is sharper in cold, when the stream freezes.
Children throw twigs on the ice. Last night's squall
Blew two huge branches in a cross on our brown turf.
A congregation of distressed silos mourn toward a
    disheveled barn.

There's an iron horseshoe on the door.

When I hear Jon Batiste sing, play piano,
See him dance, I am like an old plantation house
With ill-fitting windows letting rain in,
Loaded with ghosts,

Making the night darker over every auction block and
  big house.

What is Hidden and Hidden From

1. Azaleas lap up sunshine
   like buttonholes unbuttoned let light through
   in spurts. Both bring a smile to my lips.
   Downturned mouth turned up. Schooled
   in a finishing school teaching love, they can't claim
   high marks, love doesn't do that.
   What about an article in *The Lancet*:
   "Azaleas make people smile." An n of one
   submitted within a margin of error.

2. Who knew Claudius was a birdwatcher.
   His blue jay song made him lonely.
   Hamlet 1 was never home. Junior was in college.
   Every blue jay needs a mate. She felt
   she still had the Force of a Tarot card:
   to hold the lion's mouth open and at heel.
   Now the stay-at-home admirer
   shined the satin of her gown.

3. No albatross, no more than Jonah in holy day whites.
   Or Captain Queeg rolling dice is evil.
   No staff, no wind in the wings to repel the waters.
   The measure of sapiens might be sloth
   leading to panic: paranormal and paranoia.
   Mars' twin boys at the Forum.
   Some say Babel freed up creativity.
   Others saw purple metal pusillanimity, or a case for
      trust-busting.

4. The smell of plastic in children's urine,
   the sore that pricks sapiens into a murder
   of sleeping beauties dreaming of saviors.
   I flick away a bug, get blood on my finger.
   Like ourselves feral earth rages, like us the earth's
     best parts
   die first, the song of birds quietens.
   When next a bug lands, I'll blow it off.

There Will Be A Time When

When...

You run into a robin alongside a marsh.
She pushes out her yellow breast, her yellow
breast, proud as a penguin.

She invites you to take a ride
on her wing, until a red wing blackbird
distracts her.

Above an osprey fixes twigs in her nest
fitting up
for nativity.

When...

You run into a drive-in confessional,
rubbernecking   lined up to allay
fear in the time of covid.

Bishop Tutu like Simon/Peter or Simon Templar
(the Saint) says, "Take off your masks from the inside
out." You have to hold your breath,

forgiveness means sacrifice, Tutu's bet
about truth and reconciliation
requires a high redemption quotient.

When...

You run at a greyhound flit
along a sunset until you have to shield
your eyes.

Billy Graham told me, "Of course,
there are many ways to god." He
tore down the rope in his 1954 Tallahassee tent.
Encounters on a human scale
set safety pins
in the diapers.

When...

Triage permits cost more than carbon credits.
Nudist camps require sperm count passports.
All songs about riverbends and roads taken

or not.
Gulls drunk and flailing on the smell of beer
where beach spiders gather to gawk

at paisley jeans with holes in the knees
which signify
when...

When....

You know to stay out of the range of cannon
at the shore. Gunners wank matches
and we have war to expiate.

You wonder how much of a beating
aqua and terra take from golf clubs
and other irons.

The abscess keeps pussing up.
Hot poultices leave scars:
fitting up the earth.

Relatively Speaking

Gasoline should not be carried in plastic bags.
Leaks shorten breath. Lucky we are
that like pigs and mice
sapiens can breathe through their assholes,
which makes asthma and diarrhea
cousins once removed.

x

Snow hardens   ice drips,
dripping
not in the English culinary sense,
best wear a hat indoors
sense of domestic bliss, in
the family of man sense
of relative.

x

Wet nurses cooed over babies.
Like "little one"   "baby blue eyes."
Sounds woven for warmth
waiting on the letters of a name
not yet given.
Perhaps to be reordered to spell another:
names are for survivors.

x

For a butterfly there is no forgiving, only forgetting.
For a frog the mower is hard to take.
For a magpie there is no treasure, only glitter.
For a squirrel squirreling
there is a forest waiting to happen,
like eggs in sapiens girls
fertile flotsam and fission.

x

To be home for Akwesasne, Uyghurs, Levites, Armenians,
Palestinians, Hmong, Haratin, Sindhi, Ogoni
means to step across fossils and cough up blood
that changes the landscape. Like the cat who missed the bus
playing sax on street corners to raise the fare for a taxi.
When home is occupied like a busy lavatory
Impatience on the parallel takes few prisoners.

Why Children's Authors Anthropomorphize Animals and Flowers

1. Look at a hose
   See an elephant.
   Look at a bank
   See a carnival of magpies.
   But "as if" is hell, ask Faust
   If it is not heaven.
   In a convex mirror we can notice
   Heroic suffering.

2. Buttercups are not always friendly with daisies.
   Toads are okay with frogs
   In the grass, they feel each other's angst.
   The white board they sleep on is obsolete.
   Still they have their dreams
   Woven in the weeds of longing
           the smell is pungent
           the flower ethereal.

3. Let go your tile, your shingle,
   Imagine whiskey is a liver cleanser,
   Embrace your leaks,
   Carry your smile as wide as a sombrero.
   The alphabet still has 26 letters,
   Publish your garden,
   Lick your lips, unafraid of spit.

4. Dali painted a woman's body with drawers
    In it. To be heard like a radio or internet
    It must be turned on. The print is torn
    Across white and black teeth at the dump,
    Silent memory of shared taste at home,
    Except the accordion plays nonstop
    As if programmed. Must think it's an organ:
    Bach concertos skip my step and I wonder about that.

5. In my high school class in NE London: one Cypriot, one
        Kenyan,
    I the only Jew. We were each other's grateful presence.
    It was a lifetime. A fly lives 30 days.
    Fireflies about the same.
    Here and gone is a lifetime
    By any definition. What time for *divorce, career change,
        recovery,*
    Redemption? If redemption comes early
    Buttercups will befriend daisies.
    Toads will still do well with frogs.

I Came Upon

1. I came upon a dog shitting in the street
   On a long leash. It had no head covering,
   No yarmulka, no burka, no beret.
   But I got thinking about Israel. War is shit.
   And I'm allergic to dogs. An allergic spasm
   Could mean exposure to an aimless bayonet or
   Bullet. The kind of friendly fire that suborned Spinoza.
   And all the heretics of silence, schismatics of the whispered.

2. The juice of unripe fruit tastes like shame.
   Reports have it: sapiens is getting taller, sperm count
   Is falling off. It›s all up and down. Will we ever
   Put Humpty together again? Began today killing
   An ant in the bathroom. Checked the mousetrap.
   "Have-a-Heart" variety. Have a heart! Have a heart!
   What is an ant for? And the guns? the bombs?
   The heart survives outside the body, don't you know?

3. Do no harm, and then some.
   On a high diving board sunshine obscures
   Shallow water. Watch out!
   The barn door swings on the way out.
   I keep wondering, if we give back,
   What did we take?
   Sacrifice is necessary. Chew before you swallow,
   Walk before you run. Let the lesson begin.

4. Easy to condemn the rose, blossomed and fading
   Into its next promise. Easy to condemn the rose
   For the water it consumes. All in the way ideals
   Sparkle in the young.
   I am still the angry one, pulsing,
   Ready to mobilize offense. Just as if sunflowers
   Writhe in shadow when stars try to offer comfort,
   Mistaking them for selfishly colonizing space.

5. Guilt over what's been given
   Is the heart of darkness, the beat
   The beat that threatens to the point
                              of yellow stars
   That erupts in the pigmentation
                              of skins
   That oscillates with orphan understanding
                              of urges.

When I Courted Atheism in Eden

1. When I courted atheism in Eden,
    When I found religion in Jerusalem,
    When the grand Inquisitor took matches
    To Baba Yaga's hair, I cried
    For the skinny anorexic tree of good and evil.

2. Utopia is laid out in body shapes.
    Nothing wrong with geometric hope.
    Not even with hands cupped in worship.
    As long as untidy steps by bodies reaching
    For each other are loreful.

3. The trip rope is never a safe railing.
    Note the wobble and the weave,
    The shake up and the shake down.
    Was there ever a dream meant
    For all blood types?

4. No longer acne to apologize for.
    Still apology does not come as easy as guilt.
    Yes, break the branches off
    The climbing tree
    Before the kids run into its sharp edges.

5. Or, play Uno with the family.
   Cheat   everybody laughs a lot.
   The past is quickly forgotten, clipped
   Like fingernails, as if it›s not wired
   To grow back.

Flat Earth

It's been millennia
The talk of love
          (and hate)
The talk of barbarity
          (and compassion).

Twins
Born of the same labor
In one or separate sacs
Facing off
          (for enough blood).

In torpor
The foul taste of scat
The sewer smell of asparagus urine.
Back against the wall of opening:
          (flat earth)
Promising everything
To those who will lose everything.

It's been millennia of forgetting
Like slowly ripening fish.
Throw back the catch. Histories of subordination
Are only different superficially.

Articles I II and III of Treaty
Between Earth and Self
(with Preambles)

Preamble I

Blood and water   vintage
Addictive mixes will souse
You up, bring you down, open your heart,
All in timeless steps to thought,
To conscience, to dream. I doubt
It was a god who put us to sleep.
O what a figure we cut
Before we cut us down.

Article I

Be an ally to the earth
As you might be Spartacus or Horatio.
Defend the bridge, beat back the raging tiger,
The earth will be loyal to your treaty
With it. There is no in between....
Loyalty is an intimate exchange:
Not as in mercury and syphilis
More like learning that learning
Is to recognize who you are
And that she already is.

Preamble II

You know how a floating dock slides on water,
How ducks splash when they fish, how car exhaust
Throws squirrels off balance, releasing acorns
To be trodden underfoot by joggers.

Article II

Be an ally to the earth
You can download the paperwork (public license)
No more to do and do, and not to dream (Yeats).
She is weightless   no need to pump so hard.
No need to stare like that with bitter heart.
The earth will curtsy as long as you bow.
You really must bow your head.

Preamble III

Rained heavy all night
Truck tracks in the mud in the morning
Styrofoam plates in the grass
Alongside a plastic coke bottle,
ITunes still thinly thinking in the overhead cables.
Perhaps conception last night in the cabin.
In the bottle a message on the back of a ferry ticket

Article III

Be an ally to the earth.
Watch the oak and pine recline
In late winter like Greek gods at sprawling rest,
Their power delegated to you.
Don't dare think the earth is a hemorrhoid
Just because it bleeds. Bind the wounds.
She can recover from your coercion.
Look, see Gaia and Ganesha have already signed,
Scratched in the viscus of their broken eggs:
Yellow is now the color of courage.

Fiat lux!

Mapping

I like what is called mapping:
Drawing routes, light years, roads
Not yet travelled, the micro future.

I map in the color of eyes, in the color of ear wax,
Of urine, of paint chips scrapped off old barns.
I map dream tops, disappointment sheds,
Geese taking an old-fashioned walk, stigmatic
Mountain lions figuring out tri-focal lenses.

I map the tours of those who can touch a hoop
Without reaching, the limp of those who can't,
The highway trough of those who place bets.
I map the spray of disinfectant, the infection
Lining plastic shelves, zip code dice thrown about.

I map the phragmites at oases to show
how overgrowth itches remorselessly.
I map large perennial grasses, discovered America in
   slave ships.
And spread westward to celebrate Easter.

I map bees swarming children to protest their queen's
Imprisonment for pollinating on private property.
Each mom blows her breath on his face,
Adds honey to her breakfast cereal.

I map low flying planes it's difficult to see when lilacs
    bloom
Shooting bullets as if lone petals might have a will to
    cover the ground.
You could see trees swoon, flip backwards somersaults
When lilacs brown and low flying planes blast bullets
Into full bloom bodies.

And oh...
I map pilgrim's trails, see them become the vegetable and
    the grease.
I map where squirrels lift their legs like dogs
On cucumber vines.
I map lovers grazing back and forth on makeshift swings.

And oh...
I map the tremblings of monsters
Who run their mouths on emptiness
In hope some terrifying Other might make them human.

Epiphany

Why smoke Gauloises in the rainforest
After the gotcha x-ray: frayed lung tissue,
Denuded woods, siamese disasters?

Prelates of excess purloin god
The way a ventriloquist dummy parrots estranged prophets.
Like magpies who have stolen mirth

Their rasping song recalls the loss.

Marlborough Man strides across the Grand Teton
Amazon usurps a name, abuses its fundamentals
To sacrifice warehouse brawn and sinewy reach:

An atonal writhing in indignity, the fugue of despair.

Soy grease softens twigs and cigarette butts
Burn spent leaves. Plows and of course swords
Bloody with overheated desire and the freedom myth

Of choosing anything over anything else.

Biology is a slow green, history a fading yellow,
Contingency a sun-scratched red. Gauloises
Stolen along with mirth in the Magpie's claws

Rasps another stillbirth.

Being of childbearing age is tectonic
From what I've heard. A fête for those who will
What comes next.

What's what is not.

Only mothers know there was once life here.
Mothers know higher purpose in the feast of placenta,
In the soft delicate majesty of breathing,

Applause for the arrival of what they long for.

Judy and Neuroscience

1. Judy at the bar
                keeping.
Maybe neuroscience.

She knows   what
                she knows
She's seen it all.

Embrace   or avert
                depends
Depends.   Hardly fundamental
Like writing
                without punctuation...
Never know another mind.

2. Neuroscience studies monkeys
                watching
Each other through glass.

Just looking sets off the same neurons
        Like guilt, the invisible curl
        In every white lie.

Watch a pro baller feel your neurons
                  sync.
Watch a bigot kick and rage....

And the crow will lie down
With the robin.

Faust would have loved
To ask Mephistopheles if
                this is where evil begins,
Original original sin.

3. "You could use a drink" says Judy
                at a level of significance,
    "I know, just juice."

She confides: "Something happened."
You can tell
              Something happened.

"Six nights a week he's here
             I'm here
Until I take the trash out
          to the bin.
One night a week I'm home
            resting."

Lateral Formations

     plane
     falcon
     sparrow

My boy, aged 10 years,
My girl, aged 10 months,
A newborn,   10 days,
Child of a friend.

Lateral formation

the way it's said:

     spirit
     body
     mind

or, if you like
     all kinds
of   phases
     stages
     compartments
boundaries in orders of import
     or export...
It's a matter of whose who
     what's what
     and why not.

x

Try putting latex gloves
on wet hands...
It's raining
spectacles blur
fingers tangle at the joints
knuckles wish they're elsewhere.

It's like crying while laying Tefillin...
One more time. Each strap bruises,
the headpiece feels like a weight,
a losing thread...
I can see my eyeglasses shatter
just the way the shards of broken lives
sever veins: blood flood.

talk about the Red Sea,
might have been me afraid of beetles
in the seaweed, terrified of red...
a prophet could see the massacres
to come when
frantic people
        see red.

sapiens
simian
vespoid

the way children evolve fluency,
learn names, give names:
"in the beginning" all over again
      and again...

lateral formations

as often it's said:
"better dead than red"
"red sky at night"

blush
blush
     why don't you?
     I do.

Oskar Morgenstern vs Bowling Alone

No body bowls
alone.
Bowlers keep company,
teams compete.

Game theory has it:
it's all a game.
War games   sides enemied
on war footing   require
leaning
back to back.

Soldiers take a stand
leaning against each other.
not the same as leaning in
against the others.

Game theory: the game is always afoot
when bonds perforate boundaries
as if it's all sewn up.

Sigmund to Albert
(1932 "On War")

fists open
letting out water
    like a bird
with webbing
like a colander.

fashion bobs
    like a compass
to cover up desire,

until passion
    like threads
unraveling is taken up
in a chariot of fire
    like Moses.

I Twinkling

I in I am, I in I could be,
I in I once was, and I just don't know.

The prospect of contentment is quicksand.
Confidence is a grifter.

Like catching an insect on paper
Folding it as if agreed on,

For delivery to earth.
Not like putting down a pet dog.

It was a wasp.
The window screen bled.

The window was a mirror.
Regrets must go some distance.

Communion in parting moments.
Compassion for a life briefly lived.

Gone! Gone!
In a twinkling of an I.

Beauty/Truth Truth/Beauty
...and I should mention methane

1

The Komodo dragon is heading
toward extinction.
Those with fire on their breath
are known to enjoy their neighbors' ankles
singed on the outside, rare on the inside.

Evolution now in crampons
begs for mercy.
The fairground of the faithful
watching pixies gargle,

gargle up enough spit
so like the witch of the west
the faithful dissolve.
A match breaks.

Splinters infect a finger,
the box scatters
on the tiled kitchen floor
like bones in a desert.

Takes a needle—
forget the scattered matches.

2

So much written about beauty.
Bottom line: the sun on a lily
        the nightingale›s cough.
Not the butterflies pirating other flies' larva.
Not the snapping turtle eating a fish's ass.

No, the sun   the lilies   the cough
add up to: there must be truth,
        there must be sapiens solidarity—
Beautiful! Take a baby's smile,
melts your heart like snow under a heat lamp,
butter running off the plate,
like the truth.

3

Born in a ghetto
        after ghettos.
Born in a cellar
        after all the cellars are flooded.
Born at the birth of most people living
        born in wait
For what they all wait for.

Why not wait?
        your iron mask is not so heavy
To soften the mud under your feet
        methane stinks up the well-mowed grass
Congregants recognize it,
        you can see it on their faces.

At this point the poet tries to staunch the bleeding
          (reject pessimism),
Resist the drive to punish
          tell the heron you love her
Make a date.

I travel with a rose bush on the backseat.
Each overnight I water the plant, heading home.
After 300 or 400 miles
I wonder if the blossoms
that survive the bumps
feel at home in my car.

The Stickiness of Fly Paper

1. Tynedale swung
      for the King James
  George Smith broke
      the cuneiform code
  To give up Gilgamesh.
      look in that mirror!
  A universe of pebbles
      and the world a pebble in a sampler basket
  So pour water
    on the Temple steps.
  Only you
    can clean them up.

2. Oh yes, stick a pin in purgatory
      throw out hell's clock,
  Forget Dante.
      an ageing Beatrice is a delight
  To those not blinded
      by funereal trains of patients
  Dying like pins in a cushion.

  Django swings on the hillside
      looking for mountains
  Kicking up pebbles
      mistaken for a wraparound world.

3. Once poets walked with hip pistols
              and killer dogs.
   Plato's fear of poets like dung piled
              no need to fear a divine hand
   When sapiens believe in themselves.

   A child at his father's feet
              refused to move.
   The boy was stubborn
              the father too.
   On bent knee
              he asked his boy to move
   "Carry me, daddy"
              "That was yesterday, son.
   Today is later."

   The boy grew three feet in that sitting.
              he found pebbles in his pocket
   Pelted dad. Passersby called out "Bad boy!"
              "Bad boy!"
   He set out to write a manifesto
              to change the world.

4. Once priests wore "confession socks"
              to leaven the worst of sins.
   Later these became "compression socks" for blood pressure
              and pregnant feet
   To pray on   perhaps to fly on.

So turn off the toasters while you listen to the wheat moan.
        why not let new seed grow unafraid
Unseduced by addictives and promises.
        between the seducer and the seduced
Between the killer and the killed
        who is preferred by god, and by what god?
And who, you reader, me writer
        prefer
        choose
        or change?

5. When they tried god in Auschwitz
        they said he coulda shoulda.
As a proxy for humanity
        they said we coulda didn't wanna
Enough

Write no love letters for humanity
        sing no love songs
Baskets full of lotus petals
        have been heaved overboard.
Melted ice cream in the large fridge downstairs
        won't pay the bills
Debt doesn't melt...
        they also serve those
Who love unconditionally

6. They could write dictionaries
        to cook hope anew.
They could write canon
        to fire the stove
But not raise ripe fruit
        nor have the tide abate.

Might the fallen soldier tell us
    all is forgiven
Might the battered baby
    cough
And smile again.
    might the decalogue cut
With red hot zeal
    into unconscious lamentation
Sung aghast
    in guilty lofty arias
Are we not but the stuff remnants sell
    for cheap and is this all the calculus
For the meaning of god?

7. Imperial clutter tosses about in the air
    resisting sunset
On white bathroom tile.
    Until the afternoon shadow turns thick
    rising up the pole like lines of ants
On white bathroom tile.
    "endangered" "invasive" species
Both.
    bamboo is us and we are bamboo.
Watch the ragweed sneeze
    it's all so cellular
The coming and the passing through.
    the mosquito buzz from my lettuce
Could be my phone vibrating
    like a curator moving family portraits
From one room to another
    or into the gallery basement.

People say a baby's smile is only the gut.
        but what a smile
Perhaps the heart of imperial expectations.
        why else infantilize the natives
Does it matter if it's only from the gut?

Among those for whom desire is destiny
        shelf-life dreams
Easily fall between the thumb and the forefinger
        squeezing
Until the expiration date comes due
        the way Heaney talked about lives
In a continuous present.
        important to keep the digits moist
Life depends on moisture
        coming and going and coming
Breathlessly
        this is the bridge
We are all fledged on.

9. Two boys fought, brothers
        they cling until it hurts
Letting go hurts.
        so strangers are exotic
Known knowns burdensome.
        they played buccaneers and all sorts of outlaws
One was captive
        defeated by primogeniture.

The heart is where love abides
and hides.
Pumping passion into murder
none of it in the stars
Only in the bargains we effect
without comment
Wired up by Nietzsche
breathless
In the wild country of the heart.

10.   Some reported it was a crow
Noah mistook for a dove
It was a puddle after a huge rain
he mistook for a flood.
Crickets worried about one foot coming down
after another
As if malware in the brain
made him feel heavy feet in a puddle was
not so bad
So lost in hermeneutic crosshairs,
poor man was horrified
When his son saw him and Queen Anne lacey
undercover
not knowing
It was makeshift to replace his soaking briefs.

11.   A simple window
frame and sash   innocently open
Another's lifting
two birds, silent as nuns in prayer
Headlong into a marble statue of observance
with penitents silent on the floor.

Falsetto warriors trying to crash
        the sound barrier
Unbroken voices of boys
        chasing a hair with a razor
Still convinced a fallen bird
        can be raised
Just like the nuns' crucified hero.

Morning haze stretches as far as
        breath for millennia
Until it burns off
        covenants
Written in bleeding time.

Is there a doctor in the house?
        has enough blood been stored
Can we transfuse enough?
        will butterflies ever again
Let go of their overnight emails?
        someone saved a couple of cows
In Ida's Louisiana
        but rescuers can't change what is:
Try calling a cow a slave, fit it into work pants
        you'll only get a breathless moo
Vegetarian turd, and flies—

Imprisoned in hope
        they deny the stickiness of flypaper.
It's not as though water breaking against rocks
        is analogous to us
Or can we reunite after splintering
        heal enough
Not to concoct blood cordials?

No more contrapuntal crusades for harmony.
        a rose at the end of the garden
Looks like a microphone
        sounds like karaoke
Pre-recorded vernal chords
        Fuguish inside and outside of atonal
melodies
They cry out "Invent! Invent!"
        not the Ode to Joy,
But with a hop, skip, and a jump
        maybe
The dissonance of tuning up.

12.   Freedom zeal
        love zeal
Houses requisitioned by the authorities,
        a lone refrigerator
Hungry without power
        gorging on your family dinner.

Words are like twigs on a fire
        too wet they won't burn
Too dry they will burn too fast
        too many vowels they will regroup
And say something else
        again
Something else,
        some on a leash
Guiding the blind
        the police
Some chew through the strap
        run off.

13.   The boys' friend Nell rows
              winding along the canal
      As on a newborn wherry
              already lashed against the shore
      Premature contractions.
              what were you expecting?
      Old barbie dolls already cost more than an old woman's
        funeral
              and a young one's birth.
      So hedge your bets
              it's a maze no matter what
              no matter who
      Species spoilage is predictable
              madness is freedom
      Perhaps freedom is madness,
              even flies deny the stickiness of fly paper
      Pick up your sax
              and cut down the hanging trees.
      Invent! Invent!

When Earth Quakes

When Earth quakes
(St. Vincent burning)
Does it tremble with fear
Of us?
Oracular dread of what's coming
From us?
Prophetic about punishment
(thunder bolt from Krypton league)
To us?

The Earth quakes
Ready to take one for the team
If we can learn
        to listen.

Listening is the abundance
We have to share,
The shape of age is in it
(knees aching
        complaining)
Shape changing tremors.

The thrust needed for take off
Is illusive,
Confounded by the logico-paradoxo
Of blast:

To blow up the shebang.
To curse mistakes ....Oh blast!

Let's expiate.

No Bounds

She was one of those extravagantly pretty flowers
That grows free if you let them.
She trembled with the trees
When planes flew low.
Won a scholarship to college.
Majored in love. Broke records.
There were no accolades.
Love claims no credit.
In the vestibule there's a plaque
To Anonymous, like honoring
An Unknown Warrior.

Sun in a Twist

Oops
The sun came out this evening
terrified by entropy,
its own rays and cloud cover obscure
everybody's vital interest
in knowing if this ever happened before.

Two pigeons on a narrow stone balcony
are busy with each other, a soprano sax duo,
until evening is interrupted by the sun.
They have never seen each other in this light,
at this time of day. Could they be doves
fretted as they are by forgiving?

Oh to teach them Esperanto, to learn how
they consider their options.

Oops
They seem to like to wear their wingtips rolled
as they paddle their feet in warm water.

ABOUT THE AUTHOR

COLIN GREER is President of the New World Foundation. He was formerly a professor at CUNY. He has published several social science books and co-authored *Choosing Equality*, which won the Intellectual Freedom Award. Colin was a founding editor of *Social Policy Magazine and Change Magazine*, and wrote a column for *Parade Magazine* for almost 20 years. His plays have been performed off off Broadway and in regional productions. His poetry has been published in *Kosmos Quarterly*, *Tikkun* and *Hanging Loose*. This is his third poetry collection.

ABOUT THE PUBLISHER

LANTERN PUBLISHING & MEDIA was founded in 2020 to follow and expand on the legacy of Lantern Books—a publishing company started in 1999 on the principles of living with a greater depth and commitment to the preservation of the natural world. Like its predecessor, Lantern Publishing & Media produces books on animal advocacy, veganism, religion, social justice, humane education, psychology, family therapy, and recovery. Lantern is dedicated to printing in the United States on recycled paper and saving resources in our day-to-day operations. Our titles are also available as ebooks and audiobooks.

To catch up on Lantern's publishing program,
visit us at www.lanternpm.org.

facebook.com/lanternpm
twitter.com/lanternpm
instagram.com/lanternpm